D0850733

SYMBOLIC ACTION
IN THE PLAYS OF THE
WAKEFIELD MASTER

SOUTH ATLANTIC
MODERN LANGUAGE ASSOCIATION
AWARD STUDY

SYMBOLIC ACTION
in the Plays of the
WAKEFIELD MASTER

Jeffrey Helterman

The University of Georgia Press
ATHENS

Copyright © 1981 by the University of Georgia Press
Athens, Georgia 30602

Set in 11 on 12½ point Times Roman type
Printed in the United States of America

Library of Congress Cataloging in Publication Data

Helterman, Jeffrey.
Symbolic action in the plays of the Wakefield
Master.
Bibliography.
Includes index.
1. Towneley plays. 2. Mysteries and miracle
plays, English—History and criticism. 3. English
drama—To 1500—History and criticism. 4. Sym-
bolism in literature. I. Title.
PR644.W3H4   822'.1   80-18273
ISBN 0-8203-0534-0

A version of Chapter V, "Satan as Everyshepherd: Comic Metamorphosis in *The Second
Shepherds' Play,* appeared in *Texas Studies in Literature and Language* 12 (1971): 515–30.

Contents

I • The Wakefield Master

SYMBOLISM AND REALISM

The outstanding playwright of the Middle Ages probably began his work at Wakefield as a play-doctor. His
was the last of at least three different hands that composed the cycle,[1] and the following scenario of his
activities, although conjectural, represents his likely relationship to the Wakefield cycle.

By the first half of the fifteenth century a complete
cycle already existed at Wakefield, but it was pieced
out with a number of single plays borrowed in whole
or part from the York cycle. The man we now call the
Wakefield Master was probably first brought in to rework a number of extant plays in the last third or
passion group of the cycle. All of his partial revisions
occur in the group of plays beginning with the Conspiracy and ending with the Judgment. In all, including his
completely new version of the *Coliphizacio,* he
worked on eight of the eleven plays in this passion
group: *Conspiracio [et capcio], Coliphizacio, Fflagellacio, Processus crucis [et crucifixio], Processus talento-
rum, Peregrini, Ascencio Domini,* and *Judicium.* The
revisions include major additions to the Judgment
play, whose original was borrowed in its entirety from
York; a rewriting of almost the first half of the Scourging play; a new beginning for the Conspiracy play; and
a new beginning and end for the Play of the Talents.

Since the Judgment play would be complete without
the additions,[2] it seems likely that the tight grouping
of the revisions does not indicate damage to the last
third of the manuscript, but rather a desire on the part

of the guilds to make these plays more lively. To this end, the playwright seems to have specialized in colorful villains; almost all of the additions noted are speeches given to characters like Pilate, torturers, evil councillors, and devils. This is true even when the new material is praise of Christ, whose miracles are cited as evidence against him in *The Scourging*

The success of these revisions probably led to the writing of the six original plays, most of which are also dominated by memorable villains. These plays were needed perhaps because a York version was at that place in the cycle, perhaps because the extant play was simply second rate. Almost certainly these were replacements, since, as Kolve argues, a complete cycle would already have a Cain and Abel play, a Noah play, a play of the Innocents (Herod), and a Birth of Christ (Shepherds').[3] *The Buffeting,* although not required by Kolve's formulae for play selection, is almost certainly a complete revision of an original play, since the playwright's most complete partial revision is the play following it, *The Scourging*. Although the sequence of this speculation could be reversed, with the full-length plays preceding the revisions, the conclusion is the same: The playwright's first role was that of reviser, both of individual plays and of the whole cycle.

Of the playwright we know almost nothing except that he is responsible for five plays, composed in his unique stanza: nine lines rhyming a a a a b c c c b and internal rhymes in the first four lines. These plays are *Noah,* the First and Second Shepherds' Plays, the *Coliphizacio* (Buffeting), and *Magnus Herodes.*[4] The stanza signature is the primary evidence for his authorship of these plays. In addition, the powerful *Mactacio Abel* has been attributed to his hand by many critics,[5] and it is hoped that the arguments in this book about the playwright's strategy and his methods of character-ization and symbolism will strengthen the case for the inclusion of this play in the canon.

The Wakefield Master's work shows the influence of his having read and rewritten the other plays in the cycle. Walter Meyers has shown that Herod, for instance, is quite similar to such raging tyrants as Phar-aoh, Caesar Augustus, and even Satan himself.[6] Rose-mary Woolf notes that the playwright also borrows from the other cycles—the silent Christ of the *Coliphi-zacio* is familiar to him from the other plays concerned with the passion.[7] In each case, the playwright makes the figures involved more vivid and at the same time turns the historical moment into a symbolic one. He gives Herod a psychology to explain his rage even as he transforms him into the doomed Antichrist. Similarly he sets off Christ's silence by giving his tormentors end-less comments about words as they turn the silent Christ into the Word.

The work of the Wakefield Master is spliced on to the York Judgment play, whose stanzas remain essen-tially unchanged. The revision may profitably be com-pared with the work on the same theme of Hieronymus Bosch, for both artists bring a new vision to a rather stale iconography. Bosch's triptych of the Last Judg-ment (in the Vienna Academy of Fine Arts) would seem out of balance to anyone coming to it from earlier representations, like those of Giotto. Although the painting follows the standard iconography in having an earthly paradise on the left panel and a hell on the right, the central panel, which is usually given over to the division of the saved from the sinners, is devoted instead to grotesque representations of sin. Carl Linfert notes that Bosch was trying to capture this particular moment, which brings an end to time:

Here, however, the only nod to the standard iconography is the solemn apparition of Christ as Judge sur-
rounded by angels and saints in a nightly blue sky
barely touched by dawn. Even in that there is a minor
alteration: the Virgin and Saint John always fulfill the
function of intercessors for mankind before the throne
of the Judge, but here they are relegated to a post
behind and above Him. But that also has its meaning:
the time for intercession has passed. On earth one sees
nothing of the terrified astonishment that must have
greeted the word of the Judge, though it was spoken
no more than an instant before, and already His command is being executed in the direst and most terrifying manner . . . the verdict of the Lord is only the
period placed at the close of human history, which
itself has always been full of the very things that go to
make up Hell.[8]

At the moment when sin becomes its own punishment,
sin is seen in its true grotesque nature. So, for example, a glutton is seen drinking out of a barrel of
latrine waste; no more need be said about the nature
of gluttony. "Nature disfigured seems itself already a
kind of punishment, at least for those who look at the
picture not so much as punishment, though as warning
against immoderation and indulgence to the point of
satiety."[9]

The same kind of asymmetry and grotesquerie are
found in the Wakefield Master's revision of the York
Judgment. The original York play has all the symmetry that Giotto might bring to the event. The attention
is equally divided between the angels and devils (three
of each), and between the good souls and the bad (two
of each). The major point of the York play, once the
division of souls has been accomplished, is to point out
that all deeds, good and ill, directly affect Christ; that
is, to comfort the needy is to comfort Christ and to
ignore them is to ignore him. The bad souls disclaim

their guilt at first because they do not recognize this relationship of sin against man as sin against Christ.

The Wakefield Master is also interested in the concept that Christ is continually crucified by man's sins, but the sins named in the York version—"wikkid werkes, mysmevyng, sinnes, cursidnesse, covetise"— are too vague and too pallid to have dramatic impact. In his revision of the play the Wakefield Master removes the symmetry by adding a number of devils, the chief of whom is Tutivillus, a comic accuser of mankind. Tutivillus does not name, as one might expect, the seven deadly sins, but rather what the author of *The Book of Vices and Virtues* would call twigs on the branches of the tree of sin. Nevertheless, Tutivillus's colorful and highly detailed list makes sin not merely disgusting, but in fact the image of the sinner's life in hell. In this way, the same conception sought for by the York playwright is developed through image rather than statement.

Tutivillus begins with a catalog of specific sins, of which the following is a small sample:

> Yit of thise kyrkchaterars here ar a menee,
> Of barganars and okerars and lufars of symonee,
> Of runkers and rowners god castys thaym out, trulee.[10]

The multiplicity and specificity of the sins named not only serves to include all members of the audience, but also to make them see the ugliness of seemingly petty sins.

As described by Tutivillus, sinners in this life are already the Boschian monsters of the next, complete with bestial attributes and surrealistic detail. The whore's attempt to hide her foulness with the stylish double-pointed headgear of the day makes her "hornyd like a kowe." The most striking character is the overdressed dandy, often found in the morality plays,

bearing a name like New Guise or Now-a-Days. Tutivillus begins with a vivid portrait of the prancing
dandy whose well-padded clothing is complete with
male falsies:

> This laddys thai leven as lordys riall,
> At ee to be even picturde in pall
>   As kyngys;
> May he dug hym a doket,
> A kodpese like a pokett,
> hym thynke it no hoket
>   hys tayll when he Wryngys.[11]

This graphic portraiture yields to Boschian transformation in the continuation of the description:

> his luddokkys thai lowke like walk-mylne cloggys,
> his hede is like a stowke hurlyd as hoggys,
> A woll blawen bowke thise friggys as froggys
> Thys Ielian Iowke dryfys he no doggys
>   To felter
> Bot with youre yolow lokkys
> ffor all youre many mokkys
> ye shall clym on hell crokkys
>   With a halpeny heltere.[12]

The dandy seems no longer a man, for he has been
transformed by the Wakefield Master's imagination
into a grotesque—part fulling mill, part hog, part in-
flated bullfrog—all topped with elegantly coiffed
blond locks. It is the blond hair that punctuates the
description, much the same way as a pair of boots
fitted on one of Bosch's monsters produces a horror
the sharpest of claws or the clumsiest of webbed feet
cannot. The Wakefield Master insists, like Bosch with
his glutton drinking from the latrine barrel, that to be
caught like this at the Last Judgment is already to be
the image of one's fate.

  Rosemary Woolf argues that among the revisers of
the various cycles, only the Wakefield Master pro-

ceeds "without regard to the style and feeling of the already existing cycle."[13] This is to a large extent true, but it should also be noted that he, as evidenced by the revision of the Judgment play, has given his own stamp to allegoric and thematic possibilities inherent in the plays and biblical stories he is reworking.

One of the Wakefield Master's major innovations, in which he resembles both Bosch and Bruegel, is the way he changes the look of typology so that it has the appearance of realism. The playwright's use of typology therefore cannot be understood without defining the nature of this realistic surface.

Realism is an elusive term, because it fits into interlocking categories that seem to merge, although they should not. Realism is most commonly perceived as (a) a method of representation, (b) the purpose of presentation, and (c) an index of social and, therefore, literary value. The chain of reasoning is as follows: Since the plays of the Wakefield Master look more like contemporary life than those of the preceding century, their primary purpose is to present an image of the economic conditions in the fifteenth century, and furthermore, since the primary innovations involve characters from the lower social orders, the plays are good insofar as they portray these characters.

The ease by which this confusion of method and aims can be accomplished is illustrated by a classic transformation of a painting by Bruegel. There is in Vienna's Kunsthistorisches Museum a painting of the Massacre of the Innocents which is set in a contemporary village, and Herod's soldiers are contemporary soldiers dressed in uniforms of the day. There is also a copy of this painting at Hampton Court in London in which the "massacred innocents are replaced by sacks, geese, objects or animals, so that what we have is less a 'Massacre of the Innocents' than the 'Pillaging of a

Village.' "[14] Whether the copy was made by Bruegel
or a follower, the fact that it could be changed from
biblical story to contemporary journalism by the painting over of a few small objects shows how easily the
meaning of a work of art with a realistic surface can be
misinterpreted.

The same overlapping of the term *realism* occurs in
the criticism of the Wakefield Master, encouraged by
both the nineteenth-century evolutionary bias of seeing all medieval drama as progressing in realism toward Shakespeare, and by the use of the term in the
criticism of nineteenth-century literature, where artists
as disparate as Ibsen, Zola, and Gorky are lumped
together under a common heading (more often called
naturalism than realism), although they fit roughly
into categories *a, b,* and *c* respectively.

Millicent Carey uses realism to mean fidelity to contemporary life:

> The realism of these plays is equally distinctive. . . .
> In the other Cain plays there are only a few scattered
> references, as in Chester, when Cain suggests that
> what the fruit has fallen from is good enough for God.
> The Towneley play, on the other hand, is filled with
> reflections of Cain's farmer life—the condition of his
> crops, his hard toil against odds, his relations with his
> servant. The same situation holds in the other three
> plays; their foundation seems to be the realistic detail
> which appears from beginning to end. . . . He gains
> his effects through local allusions, proverbial phrases,
> references to many phases of everyday life, and by
> satire on contemporary conditions.[15]

By such criteria, Meissonier, who had a whole wheat
field trampled so that he could have a realistic model
for his painting of Napoleon's invasion of Russia,
might be considered a great nineteenth-century artist.
Carey's approach makes the Wakefield plays a good

place to search for historical insights into fifteenth-century agriculture and politics, but does not suggest any outstanding dramatic gift.

J. W. Robinson, in making a case for the York playwright's being a realist superior to the Wakefield Master, goes beyond Carey in making realism a relevant dramatic category. He sees realism as fidelity to characterization and relevance of motivation. Robinson notes, for example, that the York playwright is aware of everyday detail: "Other medieval dramatists . . . would not normally concern themselves with the temperature of the water in which Pilate washed his hand—the allegorical meaning, perhaps, but not the temperature. In such cases, it is clear that the York Realist has dwelt on the physical implications of each stage of a procedure and has constructed his dialogue accordingly."[16] This approach assumes a drama which is still primitive but is making strides toward becoming more realistic.

Typically Robinson is aware of the way in which the York dramatist creates realistic stage business, and, for an example, shows how the playwright has worked out several gatekeeper scenes to explain how Jesus gained entrance into the various courts for appearance before the magistrates. Robinson's claim for the naturalness of the scenes is valid, and he ultimately makes a claim for an early naturalism in this playwright.

To emphasize the effectiveness of the York playwright, Robinson suggests a comparison between the York *Trial before Herod* and its analogue, the Wakefield *Coliphizacio*. Robinson properly notes that the York play emphasizes Christ's role as *Homo paciens* and notes the use of the noisy oppressors of Christ to counterpoint his silence. He does not see how the Wakefield Master uses his own brand of realism far more effectively to make the same point. The Wake-

field Master carefully details the sources of the torturers' miseries in their long night's work, their struggles
with Christ's friends and their sleeplessness. Yet his
concern is not to validate the tormentors' suffering,
but to use their exaggerated complaints as a foil for
Christ's silent agony. The specific complaints reflect
ironically what Jesus has endured during the night, but
about which he says nothing. Similarly, realism, even
by Carey's limited definition, exemplified in the accurate depiction of Cain as a contemporary farmer, can
be dramatically effective because it creates empathy
between Cain and his fellow farmers in the audience.
In the chapter on *Mactacio Abel* it will be shown,
however, that the argument with Garcio, although
realistic at this level, serves primarily as part of a
scheme of characterization through action which aims
at portraying the emotional reality of Cain's loneliness. This condition, in turn, expands symbolically
throughout the play into a statement of the loneliness
of man without God.

A number of studies reject the theory that the plays
were primarily realistic. Both V. A. Kolve and Martin
Stevens criticize the idea that medieval drama was
meant to be illusionist, that is, to give the illusion of
reality. Dealing with the whole body of medieval
drama, both critics see Brecht as closer in spirit to the
medieval playwrights than Ibsen.

Kolve argues that medieval theater never was illusionist and that there was no attempt to get the audience to suspend its disbelief.[17] He insists that the sense
of game or "play" was made obvious by the very theat-
ricality of stage devices. Posters to illustrate the days of
creation or the omnipresent expositors prevented the
viewers from seeing the events on stage as real life, and
consequently they were able to stand back and look for
typological significance. Kolve compares the medieval

theater with the theater of Brecht and Becket, which is meant to engage the intellect rather than the emotions. Kolve is correct in stressing that recent critics have overemphasized realism in the plays of the Middle Ages, but it is also true that the Epic Theater of Brecht rarely remains within the confines of its theoretical intellectualism. Audiences do get emotionally involved with the fate of Grushe and Azdak in *The Caucasian Chalk Circle,* even though it was intended to be seen as a parable about collectivist farming.

In addition, Kolve argues that the presence of neighbors in contemporary costume was a major deterrent to illusionism. For anyone who has seen a friend perform in a community theater production, this seems to be an argument which works in theory only. In a good performance it is not hard to believe that your next-door neighbor is Willy Loman or to maintain that the local dentist is Torvald Helmer. Kolve's warnings about illusionism are important, but because they are a corrective to earlier pro-illusionist criticism, they oversimplify the nature of audience involvement in the action.

Martin Stevens expands Kolve's argument by emphasizing the professionalism and expense of medieval theater.[18] He shows that guilds not only bought costly properties but also made large outlays for both playwrighting and performing. Stevens denies the contention that the plays would be realistic if they could and that their failure to be realistic is due to the ineptness of amateur productions. The plays were very expensive, he argues, and we must therefore suppose that whatever they are, they are by intention.

Once he has established the professional nature of the medieval theater, Stevens joins Kolve both in rejecting the notion that the aim of the medieval theatre was Ibsenite naturalism, and in positing instead a

Brechtian alienation (*Verfremdung*) effect. Stevens, however, makes clear the duality of illusionist and iconographic modes at work simultaneously in the plays. He gives the example from the Chester plays of the use of animal posters, an iconographic device, in combination with a realistic ark. Similarly tormentors in contemporary dress surround a Jesus who is dressed in atemporal white garments until the passion sequence, when he changes to equally iconographic purple.

Stevens suggests that the audience is drawn into the action by the combination of realism and symbolism, as participants in a ritual rather than as spectators of a play.[19] Stevens's view is more comprehensive than Kolve's, but it is also important to remember that the Wakefield Master stands in the same relation to the body of medieval drama as do these two critics. From his vantage point as a later reviser of the cycles, he was able to see the duality of realist and allegoric representation and to use this duality for his own purposes. At least two of his plays, the *Prima pastorum* and the *Coliphizacio,* are ultimately about the difference between viewing things realistically and viewing them iconographically.

As with the plays' realism, the comic tone of the Wakefield Master has come under criticism precisely because it received so much praise from the early critics. The difficulties have largely developed over the question of whether it is possible to use comedy for moral purposes, rather than merely as an entertaining interlude between didactic passages.

It is to this problem that Eleanor Prosser addresses herself: "If a comic scene breaks the mood, negates the theme or destroys audience participation, sympathy, or necessary emotional response—if, in short, comedy works against the requisite effect of the play— is it not 'bad drama,' judged solely on esthetic grounds? . . . Can we not then, begin to evaluate the 'excrescent' comedy by valid critical principles rather than welcoming all comic insertions as *ipso facto* development of dramatic craftsmanship?"[20] There can be little argument with this principle, and Prosser is properly invalidating the claims of critics like Carey and Gayley, who did argue that the Wakefield Master wrote good plays because they contained funny scenes.[21] Prosser would seem to agree with F. M. Salter's summary of criteria for good medieval theater: "We should look for the same things that we always look for in the theatre: entertainment, beauty, representations of human life, the power to grip and hold an audience, and—above all—meaning or significance or, if I may say so, moral value."[22] The critics diverge, however, over the possibility of using the comic to achieve this moral value. Salter's defense of the parodic singing in the Chester Nativity plays does not fit Prosser's notion of decorum: "Would even the God of medieval England chuckle at a travesty of the announcement of salvation?"[23] This apparent rhetorical question is answered by Arnold Williams, who suggests that perhaps divine laughter would indeed greet the shepherds' heartfelt, if grating, attempt to raise a psalm of praise: "I always find this point hard to make to my students, most of whom have conventional modern attitudes towards the sacred. They cannot understand how an 'age of faith' could parody the most awesome mysteries of religion, how the adulterous cult of courtly love could have its 'ten commandments of St. Venus,' how slapstick and reverence can stand cheek by jowl. The truth is that medieval artists could do such things precisely because their belief was unshakeable."[24] The argument from belief explains how, but not why, the medieval artist could use this kind of low comedy.

In the Wakefield Master's plays, comedy has several functions which depend to a great extent upon where it is applied. When directed at evil characters, comedy lowers the intensity of evil. Thus imagery, allusion, and action make blustering Herod and henpecked Mak symbolize the Antichrist and Satan respectively, but the comic mood makes them less than terrifying and, in the case of Mak, ultimately humanizes him. The audience's laughter at these figures corresponds to the heavenly laughter at evil found even amidst the high seriousness of Milton. To quote Blake out of context, Satan is a dunce and his quest for power is ridiculous. The Wakefield Master uses burlesque to keep this idea ever present.

On the other hand, when comedy encompasses the good characters, it emphasizes their humanity. Noah, as ark-builder, imitates the Creator of the world, but the comic treatment of his work stresses the distance between man and his Maker. The screeching nativity song may be seen in the same way: comedy separates men from angels and reminds us that all human activity, as far as actual accomplishment goes, can only parody the divine. Only intervention by grace will raise man to the place where his acts are no longer comic. This is perhaps the underlying reason for the tendency toward burlesque that Williams finds in the Middle Ages: "The possibility of burlesque is always present, for it is the nature of the medieval spirit to burlesque the things it held most sacred."[25] The comic scenes, however, do much more than add distance and perspective. The Wakefield Master had discovered the point where Christian absurdity and comic absurdity meet. Like Kierkegaard's Knight of Faith, the comic artist must make that leap which makes the absurd seem connected to the logical.

Laughter is often a release of hysteria that comes

from the tremendous tension of watching an actor trying to juggle two or more absurdly contradictory roles. All comedy of disguise or mistaken identity, in particular, is rife with this tension and the resultant hysteria. Mak's hoax that his sheep is his child calls up this kind of response from the audience, which wonders if he can carry off the deception. The tension is the same as that filling a movie theater when Chaplin, armed only with a counterfeit half-dollar, relishes a steak, when we have just seen the brute of a bouncer pulverize a man who was a nickel short. Yet we hope against hope that the little man's cleverness can get him out of the restaurant in one piece. The tension breeds desire: would that it were so.

The Wakefield Master as comedian/symbolist takes his audience this final step; by the absurd logic of Christianity the joke can be true. The child *is* a lamb as the parody is transformed into the symbol. What makes the transformation work is the hysteria that the audience shares with the characters; in this example, the desire that the sheep be a child. For this reason it is not surprising that many of the Wakefield Master's characters are themselves desperate men. Like Mak, the three shepherds in *Prima pastorum* need a miracle, and they create a parody of it in their Three Wise Men of Gotham episode. They are hysterically funny as they argue over nonexistent sheep, dump out wealth they do not possess, and rejoice in midwinter fertility; yet their absurd behavior makes them and us require the nativity to make all this absurdity real. That the inept imitation of ideals was a close parody of their satisfying fulfillment in symbol was a major discovery of the Wakefield Master. An investigation of the sources and ends of the medieval urge for parody, therefore, will clarify the modes and purposes of his comic genius.

II

The medieval moralist, whose definition of the good
life was *imitatio Christi,* found the world painfully inverted, but he also noticed that this inversion often
bore a striking resemblance to the ideal. His attention
to verbal nuance made him quick to notice how slight
a twist was required to change good into evil:

> The numismatic is set before the numinous
> and the mark before St. Mark
> and less frequented
> is the altar than the coffer.[26]

Parody begins with a small change in a thing to produce its opposite, and these one-word examples illustrate the distinguishing mark of parody, the clear outline of the original in the parody. In the following
Mass, the kitchen has the attributes of divinity:

> The gut shall be my god,
> such deity the gullet seeketh
> whose temple is the kitchen
> where odors are divine, . . .
> and whose piled-high table
> is true beatitude.[27]

Even in this brief sketch the god of the parody has his
version of temple, incense, and beatitudes.

The idea that evil is a parody of good is founded
upon principles first expressed by Augustine, who
views all of this world, including its evil, as a mirror of
the divine. Augustine sees the Fall as man's first attempt at parody, "For souls even in their very sins
seek nothing but a certain likeness to God, in their
proud, perverse, and so to speak, servile liberty. Thus,
our first parents could not have been led to sin if they
had not been told, 'You shall be as gods.' "[28] It is an

incident from his own life that clarifies this concept. Looking back on his theft of pears from an orchard, Augustine discovers that evil always parodies the highest good: "All men imitate Thee perversely, when they remove themselves from Thee and set themselves up against Thee. But even by thus imitating Thee they show that Thou art the creator of all nature."[29] The creature, by aspiring to the attributes of his creator, cuts a ludicrous figure. In each case, the enormity of the error grows when contrasted with the attribute properly manifested in divinity: "For pride imitates exaltation, but Thou alone are exalted above all things. . . . And viciousness wishes its power to be feared, but who is to be feared except the one God?"[30] The analysis continues by showing how each of the sins parodies a specific attribute of God.

For Augustine, all human activity mirrors the divine image, but evil twists that image, while good is merely less distinct than the original: "Insofar as anything is good, it is good to the extent, differences notwithstanding, that it has some similarity to the highest good. And when a thing is natural, then the likeness is straightforward and orderly, but when it is corrupt, then the likeness is base and perverted."[31] Such a distinction leads to parody that is either sympathetic or antagonistic, depending on whether the imitation is imperfect or perverted. In the Wakefield plays, Noah's parody of divine rule is sympathetic, since his imitation of God as creator is merely imperfect—he lacks the strength, not the will, to order his universe. Herod's on the other hand, is antagonistic because his imitation of Christ as redeemer is perverted; he offers his "grace," for example, in the form of pence.

Antagonistic parody can have several effects. Since the parody contains an outline of the original, any perverse imitation of the divine can be a reminder of its presence and often enhances it by contrast. The parody of the Nativity in the *Secunda pastorum,* for example, provides a counterpoint for the magnificence of the true Nativity.[32] In the Wakefield plays, however, this effect is rarely immediate because the parody only gradually recalls its original. Furthermore, drama, as a synthetic medium, never makes explicit the relation of imitation to original, as Augustine does in his analytical work. Instead, the initial appearance of the parody causes two questions to be asked: Does only the imitation exist? or, less radically, Why does it exist? These questions are essential to the Wakefield Master's unique approach to his subject. Several of his plays end with the evil characters still in power, and only by the apprehension of the parody can the audience understand their punishment. The plays move from doubt to belief, so that parodies like the torturers' imitation of the Word in the *Coliphizacio* or Herod's imitation of Christ in the *Magnus Herodes* seem at first to be terrifyingly independent of their original, but gradually reconfirm its existence and consequently their own weakness. Augustine's explanation of evil as parody gives the playwright leeway to humanize his villains, since this view sees evil as a misguided, though always condemnable, attempt to rectify human fear and weakness.

The Augustinian conception of parody is closely related to typology, with the important difference that the interest in the plays, and to a lesser extent in the *Confessions* as well, is on the imperfect imitation and how it differs from its original, rather than upon what is being imitated (or, properly, prefigured) in typology. Because of this difference, parody in the Wakefield plays tends to be a symbolic medium, while typology tends toward allegory. Of the attempts to understand the meanings of comic action in the plays most have been typological[33] and tend to ignore the tone and style of the action. This allows, for example, a blundering, ineffectual Mak to be allegorized as the Devil or Antichrist. He does imitate Satan, but the fact that this is parody rather than allegory allows us never to forget his humanity.

Parody as a symbolic art is very close to the medieval concept of *figura,* and a restatement of its principles will help explain how meaning and action are fused rather than separated in these plays. The church fathers used the term to denote an event that was a foreshadowing of a future event in the life of Christ and the story of redemption. In dealing with this playwright's symbolic imagination, the factor of future time can be ignored, so that the human event may be the image of a divine action that has either followed or preceded it. This means that figures for the Wakefield Master are not necessarily *pre*figurations, but may point forward or backward to divine events. Except for this distinction, my understanding of the term follows that of Erich Auerbach: "Figural interpretation establishes a connection between two events or persons, the first of which signifies not only itself but also the second, while the second encompasses or fulfills the first."[34]

The major difference between *figura* and allegory is the historical actuality of the event or action that is the type of a divine act. Auerbach provides the following definition: "*Figura* is something real and historical which announces something else that is real and historical. The relation between the two events is revealed by an accord or similarity."[35] V. A. Kolve's important book on typology in medieval drama cites this distinction, but the nature of his study forces him to be concerned primarily with the second event.[36] In his study, he carefully elaborates the meaning of action in terms of what it figures rather than what it is. Thus, Noah is important to him because he is a figure of God the Creator. The Wakefield playwright, however, is equally concerned with the man qua man who is to some degree conscious of his symbolic role: What is the quality of life for a human being whose acts in some way and to a certain extent parallel those of his God?

Charles Singleton, who sees Dante's special kind of "allegory" as *figura,* or, to use his terminology, "allegory of theologians," elaborates the distinction: Nonfigural allegory allows one to dispense with the initial action once the hidden meaning has been revealed: "This allegory of the poets . . . is essentially an allegory of 'this *for* that,' of this figuration in order to give (and also to conceal) that meaning."[37] In opposition to the allegory of the poets stands the figural allegory of theologians. "The kind of allegory to which the example from scriptures . . . points is not allegory of 'this for that,' but an allegory of this sense *plus* that sense."[38] Singleton is at pains to point out that in the "allegory of theologians" there is no fruit and chaff. The influence of the Robertsonian critics, who examine the nonfigural kind of allegory, has prompted figural interpreters to disregard, or at least to slight, the first event once the allegory has been perceived: one need have no business with the chaff once the fruit has been garnered. Following the definitions of Singleton and Auerbach, however, both events are necessary because they reveal different things.

Although both Singleton and Auerbach stress the historical actuality of the primary event, each takes note only of the congruency and not of the disjunction between events. By pursuing the importance of the dissimilarity as well as the likeness of type and antitype, the Wakefield Master creates characters that reverberate with symbolic meanings rather than answer to allegorical ones. The tension between type and antitype is responsible for much of the action in the drama.

III

To call the playwright a symbolist is to say that he not only uses stock symbolic signs and typological meanings readily available to his contemporaries, but also creates his own symbolism through a sophisticated handling of the action of the plays. This art does not develop *in vacuo,* but synthesizes its dramatic form out of symbolic techniques present in the literature of his day. The analogues used to elucidate various portions of the plays have been chosen to show the currency in the Middle Ages of these symbolic techniques as well as meanings. An effort has been made to draw these examples as far as possible from contemporary English works rather than from the fathers, and from popular rather than learned literature, since these works were directed at an audience similar to the playwright's.

The audience's ability to appreciate symbolic action has been questioned by Arnold Williams, who notes that the average farmer—or playwright, for that matter—cannot be expected to have read Origen or Ireneus.[39] Nevertheless, as R. H. Kaske argues, the unlearned medieval audience possessed much more of patristic lore, albeit in an unsystematized form, than a modern secular society can readily imagine.[40] Owst's book on the sermon and Anderson's on the church building suggest how the "lewed" audience would acquire much of this knowledge.[41] The mysteries, furthermore, are a special case, since much of this information reaches the audience during the course of the cycle.

Thus the spectators have just witnessed Eve's disobedience when Noah's wife appears as a new beginner of blunder; they discover Herod is greeted with the same *ave* which was accorded the Christ child in the manger; and they are soon made aware that the buffeting game symbolizes the crucifixion.

The stress on patristics as the source of both the method and content of interpreting medieval allegory obscures the common occurrence of allegory in popular literature. While it is true that exegetical analysis declined in the later Middle Ages,[42] the popularity of collections of allegorized stories like the *Gesta Romanorum* and the *Alphabet of Tales* suggests that interest in symbolic readings had scarcely abated. Furthermore, the continued success of such collections as the *Tales of the Wise Men of Gotham*—one of which occurs in the *Prima pastorum*—shows that this interest did not die out even in the Renaissance. It is also noteworthy that the morals of these tales do not all point toward Christian charity, but often contain such homely "sentences" as a warning against wily or talkative women. Thus a lay allegorical tradition exists during the period of the plays. This tradition, available to the "lewed" members of the playwright's audience, often explicates scenes not unlike the Mak episode in the *Secunda pastorum* or the "Garcio as false friend" episode in *Mactacio Abel*. Popular allegory may or may not afford Christian readings of an incident, and does not demand a predetermined "sentence."

The symbolic action of the Wakefield plays is fluid rather than static so that allegorical values change through the course of a play. Worldly folly, for example, becomes the Christian folly that defies wisdom by the end of the *Prima pastorum*. The symbolism is articulated through the careful control of allusion, style, tone, and structure. The Wakefield Master is particularly aware of the interplay of scenes as a means of generating symbolic meanings. He uses scenic structure either progressively, as in the *Coliphizacio*, where Christ engages in a series of confrontations with forces that grow increasingly subtle in their denial of the Word, or contrapuntally, as in the *Secunda pastorum*, which compares and contrasts the real and mock Nativities.

Because the playwright is a reviser, many of his symbolic approaches are probably generated by his attempt to rework problems that he finds in his sources of the relationship of type to antitype or of parody to its ideal. In four of the plays—*Magnus Herodes, Mactacio Abel, Processus Noe,* and *Secunda pastorum*—one can see the playwright inverting, shading, expanding, or refining a symbolic situation. The other two plays, *Prima pastorum* and *Coliphizacio,* are critical reflections upon the process of symbolic thinking itself.

The Herod play is the most traditional in its use of the typology of Herod as Antichrist. The play is unlike the other plays in the cycle using this typology because of the elaborate detail with which the playwright works out the allegory. Such precision, however, is not unusual in the typological literature of the Middle Ages. It is unusual for the playwright to use typology not so much to show how villainous Herod is, but rather how pathetic a figure all such villainy cuts. As Herod's traditional bluster takes on the dimensions of Antichrist's doomed rage, Herod has both the realistic psychology of a frightened man who uses boastful authority as a defense mechanism, and the symbolic significance that all such tyranny, even in its ultimate form, is doomed to failure. This permits the playwright to leave out the customary defeat of Herod at the end of the play, since Herod, like Antichrist, pronounces his own doom by his many references to the coming of Christ. By matching the psychology of the protagonist to the play's allegorical value, the playwright makes his point even if the audience misses the many clues to the typology. Nonetheless, the universality of the theme can be appreciated only through the symbolic resonances.

The need to perceive an external analogy in the Herod play places a strain upon the audience, but the playwright overcomes this difficulty in the *Mactacio Abel,* which also ends with a murderer "triumphant." Although Cain is similar to Herod in the way his self-assurance hides his fear, the symbolic values are self-contained because the playwright begins with the commonplace of Cain as the archetypal "possessor" rather than with the typology of Cain as prefiguring the crucifiers of Christ. The Wakefield Master then fleshes out this archetype by giving understandable motivation to the traditional portrait of Cain as Worldly Wise Man. Cain becomes involved in a series of symbolic actions which culminate in his choice between real brother and surrogate brother. The symbolism unites psychology and allegory so that Cain's choice suits his personality and exposes the fragility of his value system. As with the Herod play, the protagonist is defeated both emotionally and allegorically even as he is externally victorious.

The Antichrist typology in the Herod play suggests a number of interesting combinations of parody and allegory. As an Antichrist, Herod *acts* like Christ, that is, he uses Christ's gestures, language, and so on, even as he *is* completely unlike him. The Wakefield Master inverts this relationship in Mak, who *acts* like Satan, while he is most un-Satanic in essence. In *Processus Noe,* the playwright examines a situation in which a character's attempt to imitate an antitype is simultaneously laudable and impossible. While Cain is faced with alternatives, the problem in the Noah play is to understand the dual symbolic role of Noah as *imitator Dei* and henpecked Adam in order to appreciate man's unique place in the fallen world.

The *Prima pastorum* is concerned with the development of the symbolic imagination itself, which it traces by following the transformation of the foolish "Wise Men of Gotham" into Christian sages. The *Coliphizacio* inverts the concerns of *Prima pastorum* by showing how various modes of blindness to symbolic values are acquired or perpetuated.

II • Cain's Foul Wrath

MADNESS AND ISOLATION IN THE
MACTACIO ABEL

Evil as a manifestation of fear or weakness fascinates the Wakefield Master. The theme recurs in his portraits of Cain, Herod, Caiaphas, and Annas, and his evocation of their unspoken terror explains why none of these villains are punished on stage. By focusing on the criminal rather than the victim in the *Mactacio Abel,* the playwright shows how the "nonpunishment" of the first murderer conforms to a subtle notion of divine justice. When the audience understands Cain's motivation, it learns that punishment lies in the deed itself. This principle, which provides the pattern for Dante's *Inferno,* finds its source in the Book of Wisdom: "That they may know that by what things a man sinneth, by the same also he is tormented."[1] The Wakefield Master sees that Cain's destruction of brotherhood itself is the thing that most terrifies him. John Gardner notes Cain's amazed disbelief in the fratricide.[2] This shock is based on the peculiar comic nature of the play. If Shakespeare has produced "dark comedies," this is "light tragedy"—the farce gone haywire. Garcio's merry entrance, "All hayll, all hayll, both blithe and glad / For here come I, a mery lad!"[3] is, after all, an invitation to watch the first murder. Despite our knowledge that Abel will be killed, the slapstick mood preceding the murder causes us to feel the same shock at his death that is found when the baby is thrown out the window in a Punch and Judy show.

The audience came to the play with some limited

knowledge. They undoubtedly knew the plot of the biblical story, remembered Cain's remark about being his brother's keeper, and had some vague idea about the sign upon Cain. Possibly they had also heard a sermon relating Cain and Abel to the City of Man and the City of God respectively. Whatever they brought with them to the play led them to believe that Cain was a villain at whom they could boo and hiss. The appearance of Garcio at the opening of the play would confirm this expectation.

The vulgarity of Cain's servant and his suggestion that some members of the audience are his master's men seem, at first, part of the conventional mockery that such characters direct at the audience. When, however, the villain appears a moment later driving a full team of four oxen and four horses, the remark has an uncomfortable aptness. The first murderer looks like any of their neighbors or even themselves—can the boy be right, are they his men? The farmers in the audience also note immediately that Cain needs help with the mismanaged team. The plough requires two men, one to hold the plough and another to drive the team. The repetition of his question, "Must I both hold and drive?" to Garcio and then to Abel indicates a choice to be made between his boy and his brother.

The one man driving the two-man team initiates the symbolic action. Like Everyman, Cain must choose the proper friend, yet the choice is not allegorical, but symbolic. Abel and Garcio do not stand for abstractions in this context; rather, the meaning lies in the rejection and choice itself. The language and gestures, the tone of voice, the stage business that Cain uses as he moves toward the murder of his brother, and the subsequent engagement of Garcio as his keeper combine to produce a Worldly Wise Man whose psychology alienates him from man and God.

The symbolic action of the play consists of two movements. The first is made up of those actions, primarily the debate with Abel over the nature of tithing and the ritual of tithing itself, which precede Cain's sacrifice and the almost concurrent murder of Abel. This movement defines Cain as the man whose name means "possession." The second movement consists of those actions following the murder, especially Cain's response to God and his use of Garcio to rationalize the sign upon him, which symbolize the moral and psychological consequences of living life as a man obsessed with ownership. The audience is involved because it is enticed in the first movement by Cain's worldliness, particularly his grudging attitude toward tithes. In the second movement, following the murder, they learn the cost of being his men.

II

The characterization of Cain, far from being simply a portrait of vulgarity in action, illustrates the growing self-doubt in the man who seeks to become a law unto himself and an island separate from the continent of humanity. This character manifests itself in Cain's claims to mastery, his worries about friendship, his need for material reassurance of his stature and, ultimately, his assertions that everyone but him is mad.

From the beginning, Cain tries to establish himself as the self-sufficient man, one who needs no brotherhood. When he does engage in any human intercourse he wishes to appear as a master among servants. Cain's entrance behind his unruly team illustrates his vain attempt to order the world alone. Although he reminds Garcio that the plough needs two men, his desire for mastery keeps him from the companionship

he needs. And despite the cry for help that is sub-
merged when he repeats the request to Abel, "Com
nar, and other drife or hald— / And kys the dwillis
toute!" (62–63) the vulgarity turns the remark into an
attempt to reduce Abel to the status of a Garcio.

Cain continually demands reverence from his team,
from his servant, and from his brother. He is enraged
because his team has "none aw" for him, and this pique
grows when his servant accepts his rhetorical question,
"I am thi master. Wilt thou fight?" (50) as an invitation
to hit him. Cain's demands for reverence ignore the
mutual respect required in the proper relationship of
master and servant. Paul clearly outlines the duties of
servants: "Seruauntis obeische ȝe to fleischli lordis with
drede and tremblynge in symplenesse of ȝoure herte as
to Crist . . . with good wille: seruynge as to the lord:
and not as to men" (Eph. 6:5, 7, the Wycliffe Bible)
and masters: "& ȝe lordis to do the same thingis to
hem; forȝeuynge manassis' (Eph. 6:9). The Pauline
epistles continually point out that mutual surrender of
the will is necessary to form proper relationships,
whether marital, filial, or domestic. Such surrender is
lacking in these two combatants, who substitute personal mastery for orderly hierarchy.

The search for mastery was a commonplace of the
literary tradition that grew up about Cain in the
Middle Ages. In the analogous French play, Cain's
desire for racial mastery over his brother's offspring
motivates both his murderous impulses and his building of a city to secure his race against all dangers.[4] In
The City of God, the source of the conception of Cain
as the man who walls himself in, Augustine explains
that the desire for mastery is an aspect of the search
for security that requires the construction of an earthly
city: "This is the nature of the worldly city: It worships
God or gods, by whose help it may reign victorious in

earthly peace, not by advocating brotherly love, but in the lust for mastery."[5]

Mastery also provides a motive for the murder in the Chester play, but there Cain's underlying concern is self-importance rather than self-protection:

> Say, thou cayteife, tho conioyne,
> wenes thou to passe me of renowne?
> thou shalt fayle, by my crowne!
> of maystry, if I maye.[6]

The Wakefield Master follows the English example in converting the tradition of Cain's mastery from racial to personal terms, but he also retains the Augustinian concern with security. Cain's need for possessions is part of this tradition. Through his acquisition of worldly goods, Cain is building the earthly city about himself. Since he denies charity, Cain fears putting himself in a position where he must depend upon the charity of others: "And it is better hold that I haue / Then go from doore to doore and craue" (142–43). Augustine's interpretation of Cain's city suggests that the need for economic security represents the quest for psychological stability: "Cain fathered Enoch, in whose name he founded the city. Earthly, that is to say, a city free from wandering in this world, a city satisfied with temporal peace and happiness."[7] The fleeting peace and happiness of the temporal city are attempts to find substitutes for the perfect tranquility and harmony which result from charity.

III

Charity requires the knowledge that all men are brothers. The inadequacy of "Am I my brother's keeper?" stems form the inability to understand the "we-ness" of mankind, as Dante is reminded in the *Purgatorio:*

For the more there are there who say "ours"—not "mine"—
by that much is each richer, and the brighter
within that cloister burns the Love Divine.[8]

Cain's failure to use any first-person plural pronouns in dealing with Abel indicates his blindness to the nature of brotherhood. On the rare occasion (301) when he does say "us" it is to implicate Abel in his improper tithing. Cain constantly worries about himself, and his vocabulary is filled with "me's:" "What nede had I my trauell to lose, To were my shoyn and ryfe my hose" (152–53)? Abel, on the other hand, continually uses "us," "we," and "our" to refer to the two of them. In his first speech (66–83), for example, first-person plural pronouns occur sixteen times. Abel always looks out for their joint good and salvation:

> Brother, com furth, in Godys name:
> I am full ferd that we get blame
> Hy we fast, that we were thore. (144–46)

Although Cain as the older brother should have responsibility, it is Abel who is his brother's keeper. In addition to his use of "we," Abel calls Cain "brother" eighteen times. The audience, of course, would not be counting, but if they had not noticed the frequency with which Abel uses the word, Cain makes the point when he calls Abel "brother" for the only time in the play. In a mocking echo, Cain calls Abel "leif brothere":

> ABELL: Leif brother, let vs be walkand;
>   I wold oure tend were profyrd.
> CAIN: We! wherof shuld I tend, leif brothere? (106–8)

The endearing adjective makes it impossible for the actor playing Cain to say these words without calling attention to them. Cain might say "brother," but never "brother dear." The audience might also notice that Cain manages to avoid using the word even in the familiar biblical phrase. "Am I my brother's keeper?" becomes "When was he in my kepyng?" (349).

The last words before the two go to make their sacrifices indicate a piece of action which crystallizes everything that the language has been saying about brotherhood and isolation:

> CAYN: Now weynd before—ill myght thou spede!—
> Syn that we shall algatys go.
> ABELL: Leif brother, whi sais thou so?
> Bot go we furth both togeder. (165–68)

Cain wants Abel to precede him, while Abel insists that they go together. The two undoubtedly maneuver for position, but it is unclear who prevails. If Cain gets his way here, the scene is paralleled later by Garcio's preceding Cain as they proclaim the king's peace.

Eleanor Prosser complains of Abel's "stuffed shirt" attitude: "It is he who points the moral, who exhorts again and again. I doubt that the author intended to satirize Abel, but the impression of a pompous do-gooder is made inevitable by the author's treatment of Cain."[9] Abel is a do-gooder, although if one calls him a good-doer, the pejorative connotation might be removed from the term. Perhaps taking on the role of *custos* for one's fellow man involves some prissiness, but Garcio illustrates what the alternative—of becoming "one of the boys"—entails. A figure of Abel's rectitude could become a target of comic irony. If his rectitude becomes rigid rather than resilient, if he is self-righteous rather than righteous, then we must agree with Prosser's estimation.

In the play, Abel does his best to make certain that Cain achieves salvation by doing his duty to God,

> Oure fader vs bad, oure fader vs kend,
> That oure tend shuld be brend.
> Com furth, brothere, and let vs gang
> To worship God. (72–75)

But he also accepts unflinchingly both his brother's vulgarity and his accusation of hypocrisy, "Let furth youre geyse; the fox will preche" (84). This is hardly the attitude of a self-righteous man.

Abel, the "do-gooder," realizes that his brother's lack of charity has isolated him and made him so suspicious that he fears all about him. His response to Cain's first barrage of vulgarity recognizes its defensiveness: "Broder, ther is none hereaboute / That wold the any grefe" (66–67). Abel attempts to aid Cain, not only by offering his own brotherhood, but also by trying to convince him that God is his friend.

Cain, with his economic point of view, thinks that God wants a fat tithe before he will share his friendship. With the feigned aloofness of those who hide their needs for fear of not being able to fulfill them, Cain tells his brother that divine friendship is none of his concern:

> ABELL: Cam, I reyde thou so teynd
>   That God of heuen be thi freynd.
> CAYM: My freynd?—na, not bot if he will!
>   I did hym neuer yit bot skill.
>   If he be neuer so my fo
>   I am avisid gif hym no mo. (257–62)

Abel's efforts, rather than evidencing the "stuffed shirt" attitude Prosser suggests, represent an attempt to bend his brother's inflexible materialistic approach toward God.

Cain turns away from God's friendship with the petulance of a schoolboy who snubs, for fear of rejection, a group he wants to join:

> Com furth, Abell, and let vs weynd
> Me thynk that God is not my freynd;
> On land then will I flyt. (301–3)

By spurning this greatest of friendships Cain condemns himself to exile. Although unable to accept brotherhood because of his need for mastery, and unwilling to believe he can find divine friendship, the lonely Cain still searches for a "friend." This search ends pathetically when Cain requests aid to bury his brother.

Cain asks Garcio to help him hide the body, but Garcio refuses. The request assumes symbolic significance in the light of a common medieval story. In the tale, to request someone to help bury a body was a test of a true friend. A father whose son tells him that he has many loyal friends advises the son to test his friends in the following manner: "Take and sla a calfe & lay it in salte. And when þi frende commys vnto the, tell hym þat þou haste slayn a man & pray hym for to go berie hym privalie 'þat þou be not suspecte, nor I nowder; And so þou may safe my life.' "[10] The son follows his father's advice and is rejected by all of his "friends," and the "body" remains unburied until he takes it to his father's one loyal friend. This test of a friend explains the final irony of Cain's loneliness. After rejecting Abel's proffered love, he must seek friendship with the worthless Garcio: "Bot were Pikeharnes, my knafe here, / We shuld bery hym both in fere" (382–83). That this is the first time that Cain has mentioned any kind of togetherness reveals the depth of his inability to understand brotherhood or friendship.

IV

Self-imposed isolation forces Cain either to acknowledge his own madness or to assert the madness of everyone else. The choice of the second alternative

requires Cain to establish the legitimacy of his own
sanity and to reject everything he doesn't understand
as lunacy. The tradition of Cain's madness was part of
the attempt to understand his special protection. Hugh
of Saint Victor finds the torment caused by Cain's
conscience so overwhelming that he envisions the pro-
tecting sign as the physical manifestation of insanity:
"A sign upon Cain, that is a trembling of the limbs, as
if of a maniac, that is, of a madman."[11]

Cain's imputation of madness to others by way of
defense is widespread in medieval drama, and occurs
in both the *Ludus Coventriae* play and the French version. The defensiveness of this attitude is evident in
the Wakefield play, where Cain assures himself by his
ability to count his goods that he is sane even as he
calls Abel mad:

> I hold the woode.
> Wheder that he be blithe or wroth,
> To dele my good is me full lothe. (159–61)

Cain's continual insistence upon his own sanity suggests that he protests too much. Despite the disorder
in his ploughing, he uses that business as a foundation
for reason:

> Shuld I leife my plogh and all thyng,
> And go with the to make offeryng?
> Nay, thou fyndys me not so mad! (91–93)

As has been suggested earlier, Cain's universe is pre-
cariously balanced on his own economically oriented
logic, and anything that threatens this logic must be
rejected.

After heaven spurns Cain's sacrifice, he extends the
charge of madness to God himself in order to protect
his own claim to sanity:

> Whi, who is that hob ouer the wall?
> We! who was that that piped so small?

> Com, go we hens, for parels all;
> God is out of hys wit! (297–300)

Cain hears, but refuses to listen to the "still, small
voice" that tries to moderate his rebellious spirit. We
may infer from the mention of a voice that "piped so
small"[12] that the actor who plays God is to respond
calmly to Cain's ravings. That Deus, instead of com-
manding or threatening, questions and exhorts in response to Cain's curses, supports this inference. Cain
expects wrathful condemnation of his meager offering,
as he later expects eye-for-an-eye punishment for the
murder, and his blasphemy exposes more bewilderment than contempt.

The consequences of the murder create the final
madness for Cain. Ambrose chooses the moment of
Cain's denial of brotherhood to pinpoint his madness:
"I know not, am I my brother's keeper? 'Oh! execrable
madness!' "[13] In the play, Deus chooses the same moment to bring all of Cain's accusations of madness down
on his own head: "Caym: When was he in my kepyng?
/ Deus: Caym, Caym, thou was wode" (349–50). Cain's
refusal to accept God's judgment characterizes the man
whose world goes by his own rationale: "Yei, dele
aboute the, for I will none, / Or take it the when I am
gone" (356–57). On the surface, Cain does not seem
fazed by the possibility of death. Rather, he tries to
maintain the semblance of control by deciding both his
punishment and the place he is to be buried:

> And whereso any man may fynd me,
> Let hym slo me hardely, . . .
> And hardely, when I am dede,
> Bery me in Gudeboure at the quarell hede.
> (363–64, 367–68)

For a moment, the repetition of the emphatic
"hardely" masks the desperate tone in Cain's voice.

The self-destructive cry teeters between blasphemous boldness and suicidal despair. The air of bravado allows the audience to sympathize momentarily with this bold but misguided attempt to deal with an incomprehensible universe. The allusion to the quarry at Gudeboure would also involve the audience in Cain's tendency to transform the sublime into the familiar.

Cain logically expects eye-for-an-eye punishment, but receives instead a curse which manifests itself as a protective sign. In order to place it in the materialistic terms he understands, he has Garcio join him in announcing that the king's peace has been granted to them. The plan backfires, as Garcio becomes the mocking voice of conscience and corrects all Cain's lies. Garcio's mocking "protection" turns Cain's search for peace into a nightmare.

The unpredictable wit of Garcio adds to the tension of the situation. Although the mockery is comic, the audience would probably share Cain's anxiety as to whether his new ally will keep his secret. Garcio's responses range from a bad echo, "browes" for "oyes," to a remark about food which seems on the verge of giving the game away, "Yey, cold rost is at my masteres hame" (422). The hint seems to lapse innocently into a complaint about his upkeep, but just at the moment when Cain seems safe, Garcio violates the spirit of his agreement while holding to the letter. "CAYM: Loke no man say to theym, on nor other— / GARCIO: This is he that slo his brother" (433–34). By craftily finishing Cain's sentence, Garcio lets the word out while grammatically supporting Cain's lie.

V

Cain's madness stems ultimately from his inability to grasp the logic of charity. In spite of the importance of this virtue in the Middle Ages, even Dante needs Vergil's careful guidance before he understands the good that grows greater by giving. The explanation occurs in the circle of Purgatory, in which Cain's voice is heard: "Everyone that findeth me shall slay me."[14] Dante's bewilderment displays the wordly point of view of Cain the businessman:

> How can it be that a good distributed
> > Among a greater number of possessors makes them richer
> In it than if it were possessed by few?[15]

Vergil's explanation of a good that grows by giving would completely mystify Cain. For him, a gift can have value only if it can be weighed and measured. He does not understand that the tithe is a reminder that man is the steward of God's goods. The tithe is not a tenth of what man has earned, but symbolizes a tenth of what God has given man. Abel knows that the tithe is only a partial payment of an infinite debt: "Gif we hym parte of oure fee" (76).

Throughout medieval drama Cain is a bargainer who does not think it unfair to expect a good return on his investment. In the Chester play, he goes so far as to suppose that some day God might be *his* debtor:

> I hope thou wilt quite me this,
> and sende me more of worldlie blisse,
> els, forsoth, thou doest amisse,
> and thou be in my debte.[16]

In the Wakefield play, the tithing is a major piece of stage business, in which Cain not only chooses the worst sheaves for God but also engages in the kind of sleight of hand that would be expected from shady businessmen. During the elaborate counting sequence, Cain handles the sheaves with the skill of a short-change expert so that God gets less than his tenth. As he completes his tithing with his eyes closed, it must be obvious to all that his skilled hands can leave God the worst sheaves without looking.

The tithing is a business transaction for this sharp operator, and he will not overpay his debt by even a handful:

> Now and he get more, the dwill me spede!—
> As mych as oone reepe—
> For that cam hym full light chepe;
> Not as mekill, grete ne small,
> As he myght wipe his ars withall.
> For that, and this that lyys here,
> Haue cost me full dere. (234–40)

Garcio and Cain always follow this economic system. Whether farthing for farthing or blow for blow, there is an Old Testament one-to-one equation in all their dealings. Thus, when Garcio promises Cain a return smack in the head, he assures him that it is an equitable reimbursement: "Yai, with the same mesure and weght / That I boro will I qwite" (51–52). The economic motif of the Garcio-Cain exchange of blows foreshadows the central event of the play. The murder of Abel is also the repayment of a debt: "We! na! I aght the a fowll dispyte, / And now is tyme that I hit qwite" (314–15). While the beating of Garcio previews Abel's murder, the difference between Garcio and Abel is implied in a reminder of Christ's admonition to turn the other cheek:[17] "Caym: That shall bi thi fals chekys! / Garcio: And haue agane as right!" (48–49). Abel, in the same situation, receives his brother's wrath as mildly as he took his verbal buffets. The Wakefield Master connects the two scenes by having Cain strike his brother down with the "cheke-bone" of an ass.

The Wakefield playwright does not forget that the murder of Abel is a type of the crucifixion,[18] the moment when Christ paid all the debts of mankind. Cain's calculating mind ignores the statement about the debt he owes Christ that is hidden in his expletive:

> My wynnyngys ar bot meyn:
> No wonder if that I be leyn,
> Full long til hym me meyn.
> For bi hym that me dere boght,
> I traw that he will leyn me noght. (111–15)

Cain's lack of charity is reflected in his vulgarity. The foulmouthed insults made by Cain and Garcio help characterize them as men destined for Hellmouth. Ephesians warns that not only is foul language without profit, but the men who use it will be unfit to walk in the sweet odor of Christ's sacrificial love. Eleanor Prosser dismisses the low comedy of the play out of hand: "Here the prologue is a ranting secular speech that has two purposes: to prepare the audience for Garcio's contentious master and for a comedy. Cain enters, ploughing, cursing his mare—from entrance to exit he is always a thoroughly vicious lout, as in the York version and in addition he is vulgar."[19] Although Garcio's speech is both ranting and vulgar, it has purposes beyond those suggested here. Throughout the play, vulgarity associates filth, especially anality, with the Devil. Garcio begins by announcing two possible fates for the rowdies in the crowd:

> Be peasse your dyn, my master bad,
> Or els the dwill you spede.
>
> ....
>
> But who that ianglis any more,
> He must blaw my blak hoill bore. (3–4, 6–7)

The connection between anality and the Devil is not uncommon in the Middle Ages. Dante has a twelve-line epic simile for a fart in the circle of the barrators (sellers of secular preferments),[20] and Chaucer begins his tale about the dividing of a fart with an image of an anal Hell:

> 'Hold up thy tayl, thou Sathanas!' quod he;
> 'Shewe forth thyn ers, and lat the frere se
> Where is the nest of freres in this place!'[21]

For the medieval poets, anality connotes particularly love of "filthy lucre."[22]

In *Mactacio Abel,* Abel opposes the hellish filthiness of Garcio and Cain by making purity in language and action the basis for the worship of God. Two other Cain and Abel plays also stress the need for cleanliness in making sacrifice. In the *Ludus Coventriae* Abel admonishes Cain:

> Remembryng to be clene and pure
> for in mys-rewle we myth lythly fall
> a-ȝens hevyn kynge.[23]

The Chester Cain wrongly offers the grain which has gathered the dust of the roadside, and that for the wrong ends:

> This earles corne grew nye the waye,
> Of this offer I will to daye;
> for cleane corne, by my faye
> off me getts thou noughte.
>
> ....
>
> I hope thou wilt quite me this,
> and send me more of wordlie blisse.[24]

In the Wakefield play, Abel also links cleanliness with freedom from the devil's snares:

> And therfor, brother, let vs weynd,
> And first clens vs from the feynd
> Or we make sacrifice. (78–80)

Cain inverts the idea of purity with a pun on "far-thing" and "farting" also used by Chaucer. In the Summoner's Tale, the greedy friar cannot see how the parts of a shared good can be greater than when it is whole:

> What is a ferthyng worth parted in twelve?
> Lo, ech thyng that is oned in himselve
> Is moor strong than whan it is toscatered.[25]

The pun, hidden at this point, is later elaborated when the divided farting becomes the reward for *cupiditas*.[26] Like Cain, the friar does not know that charity is the one thing that is stronger when divided than kept to oneself. He eventually gets exactly what he asks for:

> And whan this sike man felte this frere
> Aboute his tuwel grope there and heere,
> Amydde his hand he leet the frere a fart.[27]

This is the "ferthyng" to be divided in twelve, to the bad luck of the friars.

A similar jest should be expected from Cain. He has offered five anal insults in the dialogue preceding his assertion that he owes nothing to God, since "yit bor-owed I neuer a farthyng / of hym" (99–100). Besides, even if he had, he has paid it back: "My farthyng is in the preest hand" (104). Cain has given the Lord what is of the least possible value, and the pun suggests Cain's ill will makes his offering worthless. Cain does not know the Psalm which evaluates burnt offerings: "But forsothe in brent sacrifises thou woldest not de-liten. Sacrifise to God, a spiritt holly trublid; a contrit herte & mekid, God, thou shalt not despise" (Ps. 51:18–19). When Cain gives his offering with a bad will it is a farting; only when it is given with a good will is it a farthing.

Cain not only grudges his tithe to God, he also has no charity towards man:

> The dwill me spede if I haue hast,
> As long as I may lif,
> To dele my good or gif,
> Ather to God or yit to man,
> Of any good that euer I wan. (135–39)

He values man as he does God and has turned his back on humanity: "By all men set I not a fart" (369).

Cain's sacrifice fails in terms of the filth-anal imagery which dominates his thinking. From the altar comes the objective correlative of Cain's attitude towards God:

> Puf! this smoke dos me mych shame—
> Now bren in the dwillys name!
> A! what dwill of hell is it?
> Almost had myne breth beyn dit;
> Had I blawen oone blast more,
> I had beyn choked right thore.
> It stank like the dwill in hell.
>
> ....
>
> Com kys the dwill right in the ars! (277–83, 287)

The numerous curses in the Devil's name suggest that the same props used to make the smoke for the Hellmouth would be used for creating the smoke and stench for Cain's sacrifice. The familiar sulphurous odor rising from the altar would remind the audience that Cain's tithing has become as worthless as his farthing.

Abel's sacrifice, on the other hand, is as clean as the heart that gives it: "Godys will I trow it were / That myn brened so clere" (320–21). Scripture explains the difference between the stench of Cain's sacrifice and the purity of Abel's: "And walke ȝe in loue: as crist loued us, and ȝaf himsilf for us as an offrynge and a sacrifice to God: in to the odour of swetnes" (Eph. 5:2). The commentators agree that "this odor most sweet to God is charity."[28]

Ambrose divides human mentality into two classes:

the mind of Cain, whose worldly wisdom ascribes all things to human wit, and the mind of Abel, which distinguishes between creature and creator and submits all things to divine governance.[29] Unlike the church fathers, however, the Wakefield Master does not predetermine the role of Cain: He is free to choose between Abel and Garcio. The playwright closes the play by exposing the irony in Cain's choice. Cain had treated Abel like a servant—by making him precede him, by ordering him to do the servant's job of holding the plough, and by suggesting his sexual habits were those of a farm boy ("go grese thi shepe vnder the toute" [64]). Now Cain discovers, to his sorrow, that Garcio has become his "brother."

After the murder, Garcio and Cain go forth together, with the boy mocking his master. In this ironic situation, Garcio becomes Cain's keeper, the role which Abel sought but was denied. At this point Cain dimly perceives the identity of Garcio as his surrogate brother:

> The dwill I þe betake;
> For bot it were Abell, my brothere,
> Yit knew I neuer thi make. (441–43)

The food imagery Garcio uses in mocking Cain emphasizes and serves as a counterpoint for Cain's failure to understand the sacrifices. For him, the burnt offering is nothing more than the loss of so much food: "No wonder if that I be leyn" (112). Cain is traditionally worried about getting his fill. In the *Ludus Coventriae,* he says that instead of going to the sacrifice, "I had levyr gon hom well ffor to dyne."[30] In that play, Cain's argument for not sacrificing is founded entirely upon the logic of a glutton:

> What were god þe better þou sey me tyll
> to ʒevyn hym awey my best sheff,

and kepe my self þe wers
he wyll neyther ete nor drynke
Ffor he doth neyther swete nor swynke
þou shewyst a ffebyl reson me thynk.[31]

Tertullian takes issue with such men, who think that God will miss a meal if they do not give proper sacrifices:

We have spoken of the rational institution of sacrifices, as calling away their homage from idols and to God, and if he in turn rejected them, saying, "What is the multitude of your sacrifices to me?" he meant nothing else to be understood than that he did not require such sacrifice for himself. "I shall not drink," he says, "the blood of bulls"; and elsewhere he says, "The everlasting God shall neither hunger, nor thirst." Therefore he turned toward the offerings of Abel, and the sacrifices of Noah were sweet to him. Yet what joy could he have from the entrails of sheep, or the odor of burning victims? But the simple and Godfearing heart of those offering what they had received from God made the sacrifice pleasing both as food and as a sweet odor to God, who did not require what was offered, but that which prompted the offering—the sense of the honor of God.[32]

Instead of a God that neither hungers nor thirsts, Cain faces the ravenous Garcio at the end of the play.

> CAYM: For thay ar trew full manyfold.
> GARCIO: My master suppys no coyle but cold.
> CAYM: The kyng wrytys you vntill.
> GARCIO: Yit ete I neuer half my fill.
> CAYM: The king will that thay be safe.
> GARCIO: Yey, a draght of drynke fayne wold I hayfe.
> (425–30)

Garcio's commentary on Cain's version of justice is a worldly parody of the beatitude, "Blessid ben thei that hungren and thirsten riȝtwisnesse; for thei schulen be fulfillid" (Matt. 5:6). This is a proper litany for these two worldly brothers.

When Garcio mocks, "My stomak is redy to re-
ceyfe" (432), he becomes for Cain the equivalent of
the sacrifical altar, which also was ready to accept
Cain's offering. The phrase recalls Cain's irate wish
that Abel were the altar for his foul sacrifice: "I wold
that it were in thi throte / Fyr, and shefe, and ich a
sprote" (289–90). The pair even conceive of Abel's
death in terms of food imagery. Since neither of them
understands anything of the spiritual, the joking "yey,
cold rost is at my masteres hame" (422) fits the dead
body precisely.

As in both *Magnus Herodes* and *Coliphizacio,* there
is no manifest punishment for advocates of the material world, while those on the side of Christ seem to
suffer unavenged. Through subtleties of imagery and
characterization, however, the Wakefield Master reminds his audience that the triumph of evil, which is in
this world alone, must and can be endured. Cain's
triumph is cold comfort. We last see the would-be
master of his brother with the sulphurous smell of his
sacrifice still rank about him. He has become his servant's brother and the butt of his jokes as well, and his
vain attempts to rationalize a universe of illogical love
certify his own madness.

III · *Processus Noe*

HENPECKED MAN IN THE IMAGE OF HIS MAKER

In the *Mactacio Abel,* the Wakefield Master weaves together a collection of traditional material about Cain to produce a character whose actions are both humanly motivated and symbolically significant, but at no point do these different values clash. Instead, Cain's fearful worldliness shows the audience what it is to be a citizen of the city of man. In the *Processus Noe,* on the other hand, the playwright allows figural and human values to play against each other so that the counterpoint—between the typology and humanity of Noah, between the dignity and worthlessness of man, between crude comic and graceful liturgic styles of composition—produces a complex statement about man's place in the eyes of God.

During the course of the Wakefield Noah play, a viewer might be made uneasy by the contrast in style between the dignified opening of the play and the boisterous struggle between Noah and his wife. Had that person been to York to witness their cycle of plays, he would recall that a similar contrast of styles caused no such uneasiness. Further reflection would reveal the reason for his lack of discomfort at the York performance—at York there were two plays. The first, put on by the shipwrights, featured a dignified Noah who talks to God and then builds the ark under his direction; and a second, performed by the fishermen and sailors, which centers on Noah's struggle with his

shrewish wife about boarding the ark. At York, Noah
had been played by two different actors whose roles
were of different gravity. They were probably costumed differently, possibly in the respective garments
of guild members who performed the plays, i.e., Noah
as a shipbuilder in the first play and as a sailor in the
second. They might also have been costumed to reflect
the loss of dignity suffered by Noah in the second play.
In this case, Noah would wear the simpler, more timeless costume associated with Jesus, Mary, and the
apostles[1] in the first play, and contemporary garb in the
second. The use of atemporal in contrast to contemporary costuming can be seen in Bruegel's "Christ Carrying the Cross to Calvary." It is also conceivable that
Noah in the second play would be clad in the proverbial
Stafford blue of henpecked husbands (whose wives
beat them black and blue). The wife in the Wakefield
play mentions such a garment, and it is illustrated by
Bruegel in his "Netherlandish Proverbs."

The point is that the Wakefield playwright, who had
been to York (or at least had read the York plays) has
made one play out of two, but has combined the two
versions of Noah without allowing himself the luxury
of two actors or two costumes. The playwright has
not, however, allowed the seams to disappear, as anyone listening to the varying cadences of the play would
realize. The Wakefield Master has combined the two
York Noahs into one, and he wants his audience to
see both the two and the one.

A rough statistical analysis of the play shows some
sources of the difference in rhythm and cadence which
corresponds to the differing subject matter of the two
parts of the play. These differences may be as conscious on the part of the playwright as the use of the
word "brother" or "we" instead of "I" in the *Mactacio Abel,* or they may result from a more subliminal

sense of the appropriate voice for the appropriate scene.

The speeches in the part of the play that corresponds to the York shipwright's play are longer and are made up of longer verse lines and more complex sentences than those that come from the part that corresponds to the fishermen's and sailors' play. In Noah's prayer, for example, the sentences, with modern punctuation, are four or five lines long, whereas later they are often two or three lines long. The sentences are also more complex, through the use, especially, of apposition and parenthesis. The long lines of the nine-line stanza are often hexameter or even heptameter, and the short lines are usually trimeter in Noah's prayer, while later in the play the stanzas are often composed of pentameter and dimeter lines. This results in large part from a difference in vocabulary, which in the first part is far more Latinate and less colloquial than in the second. For example, the first nine-line exchange between Noah and his wife contains only three words of more than one syllable ("euer, belife, veray"). Noah's prayer, on the other hand, averages twelve words of two or more syllables per stanza, and many of them are distinctly Latinate in origin. All of these differences represent a change in cadence and tone that would be evident to a perceptive listener.

II

The York shipwrights' play begins with God's disappointment in man, whom he had made in his image and established as lord and sire of all middle earth. The Wakefield Master also uses this crisis in God's estimation of man to contrast the present dim state of man with the bright promise of his creation, but he

chooses to present it first from the mouth of Noah.
This shift in speakers makes Noah's prayer similar to
Psalm 8, both in its vision of the created universe and
its wonder at the nature of man. Like the psalm,
Noah's prayer moves from the majesty of God and his
heavens to the creation of man, the relation of man to
the angels, and the insignificance of man on earth.
The psalmist also wonders how man can be worthy of
his maker and the place to which he has been raised:
"For I shal see thin heuenes, the werkis of thi fingris;
the mone and the sterris, that thou has foundid. What
is a man, that myndeful thou art of hym; or the son of
man, for thou visitist hym? Thou lassedest hym a litil
lasse fro aungelis; with glorie and worshipe thou crou-
nedest hym; and settist hym ouer the werkis of thin
hondys" (Ps. 8:4–7).[2]

To the question, "What is man?" most of the medieval exegetes responded with a description of man's
frailty joined with his divine similitude: "What is man?
How great and how worthy to Thee? Yet I see him
frail, of no value, and unworthy of Thy consideration,
but because of his fault, and not his nature: because
Thou created him in Thine image and likeness. . . .
Through disobedience he went far from Thee, and
came into a far-off place; but Thou, through Thy
mercy, mindful that he was created like Thee by Thy
wisdom, called him back through the obedience of
Thy Son."[3] It is this double image of man that the
playwright develops in his characterization of Noah,
and an understanding of this role will answer the ob-
jections of E. K. Chambers: "In the Noah, the biblical
theme of the salvation of mankind through the preser-
vation of a single family who are ultimately to produce
the Redeemer, is transformed by this writer into what
can only be called a *fabliau* of the recriminations and
bouts of fisticuffs which take place between Noah and

his wife from the first building of the ark to the ultimate return of the dove."[4] In complaining that the
play fails to project its biblical theme, Chambers ignores the first third of the play (Noah's prayer and
God's answer), apparently because he assumes a crude
division of the play into edifying and amusing scenes.

If a case is to be made for the integrity of the play,
it will require some kind of symbolic reading of the
Noah-Uxor scene that not only develops the themes
introduced in the dialogue between Noah and God but
also explains the difference of tone between these two
scenes. Several studies have dealt with the meaning of
the comic action. Alan Nelson and V. A. Kolve ignore
the characterization and comic tone of the scene to
emphasize its allegory. Nelson limits the possibilities
open to the dramatist: "The playwright's job was not
to hypothesize Noah's probable reaction to God's
strange command, but to make the full significance of
the event clear to his audience."[5] Nelson knows that
Noah was a type of Christ and argues that the play's
significance lies in its prefiguration of Christ's perfect
obedience at the Crucifixion. He cites a comparable
example in the continental *Mystère d'Adam,* but that
play includes a direct reference to the Crucifixion.[6]
Noah was a common figure of Christ for the Middle
Ages, but no evidence from the Wakefield play indicates that he is one here.

V. A. Kolve finds an analogy more appropriate to
this particular Noah play. By starting with the action
rather than the antitype, Kolve can point out: "God's
great world is turned upside down just as is man's little
world, and for the same reason: proper *maistrye* has
been destroyed. Just as fallen man is rebellious to his
master, God, so too is the wife rebellious to her husband, and only when the proper human relationship is
re-established does the universal order begin to recon-

struct itself."[7] Kolve's analysis of the typology is accurate, but because he is dealing with the importance of the Noah story rather than with this Noah play, he must necessarily skirt some major critical problems involved in his reading. These issues are dealt with but not fully explicated in John Gardner's study of the importance of Noah's humanity and the comic tone of the play.[8]

The application of figural readings to medieval drama, and especially English drama, presents a problem, because the action in the play often parodies as well as prefigures the divine action. If we provisionally accept Kolve's analysis of the figure involved, it follows that Noah's boisterous and inconclusive attempts to subdue his wife represent God's punishment of mankind. Although this is true in a qualified way, reading Noah's beating of his wife only as prefiguration would upset the motif of disobedience by portraying God's anger in the wrong light. The medieval exegetes emphasize that divine wrath has no substantial similarity to human anger. Rabanus Maurus, elaborating an idea of Augustine's, explains the difference:

> Can repentance or a troubled heart belong to God? The wrath of God is not a disturbance of his mind, but a judgment ordained as a punishment for some sin; his consideration and reflection on changing events is certainly an unchangeable reckoning. God does not repent or lament his deeds as man does; for him there is altogether as much a fixed knowledge of all things as a certain foreknowledge, but the holy Scripture employs words familiar to our understanding, so that it may fit itself to our insignificance, insofar as we may know unknown things from known.[9]

The playwright is aware of these distinctions and capitalizes on them in developing his theme: Even as Noah imitates his Creator, he also parodies him, because this is *man* acting in the image of God.

The Wakefield Master accentuates this dual role, first by placing Noah in meditative and *fabliau* situations which expose his hero as ideal and average man respectively, and then by counterpoising patterns of imagery which link Noah antithetically to both God the Creator and Adam the first mortal man. This double context constantly reminds us that beneath the divine stamp the flawed man stands out conspicuously. This tension—between Noah as patriarch who symbolizes God's fatherhood of man, and Noah as uxurious husband who can scarcely control the most trivial events—underlies most of the dramatic action.

The play is divided into three scenes: the dialogue between Noah and God, the battle between Noah and his wife about boarding the ark, and the harmony on the ark that betokens the end of the flood.[10] These scenes are varied in tone and mode so that they can, in turn, introduce, describe, and resolve the problem of man's worthiness in the eyes of God. The first scene is expository and didactic; it asks questions about the nature of man and introduces the themes and images that will be found in the scenes that follow. The second scene is figural in mode, but its comic tone explores the relation of type to antitype rather than simply figuring forth the divine event. The comedy emphasizes that this is flawed man doing his utmost to act in his creator's image. In the final scene, the mode changes from *figura* to *exemplum* and the farcical tone is replaced by warm domesticity. The behavior of Noah's family, at this point, sets an example for the family of man.

III

The first scene presents the parallel voices of Noah and God, which at first are not speaking to each other.

Noah, below, praises God, admires his creation, loathes its corruption, and prays for salvation. The response, however, is not made to Noah, but to the audience. Noah is left vainly awaiting an answer, while the audience hears God echo Noah's assessment of human corruption. For a minute, it seems that their very agreement will keep man and God as far apart as they are on stage, with God above, as he had been in the *Mactacio Abel,* and man below. Throughout God's first speech, the actor playing Noah finds himself in the uncomfortable situation of having nothing to do. He remains kneeling in prayer, but not hearing the voice of God. Finally, God does respond. He descends, by machine or stairs, to answer Noah personally.

This breakdown of the infinity that separates man and God presents man as a lump of clay made in the image of God. The scene introduces the major themes of the play—the creation of the universe by the power of the Trinity, the fractiousness of man in obeying his creator, and the notion of sovereignty as the proper relationship of God and man. The apparent contradiction between the present corrupt state of man and the idea that man is made in God's likeness plagues the playwright. The vivid imagery of man wholly encompassed by the coordinates of time and matter projects the Wakefield Master's concern with this contradiction. The contrast between creature and creator underlies the argument of the first two hundred lines of the play because upon it rests the importance of man in the eyes of God.

Man's salvation is a central issue in the play because the Flood was seen as a fulcrum of human time, the second of three great judgments which were to correspond to the three persons of the Trinity: "You should know that the judgment of the one Trinity is triform. The first, of course, when the devil was cast out of

heaven and the last likewise when at the end of the
world he will be thrown with his angels and evil men
into the eternal fire: in the middle of this, when the
flood was brought on the world."[11] The first and last
of these judgments represent the termini of mankind's
moral life, but the Flood stands in the middle of human time.

The insistence (a half a dozen times) upon God's
triune nature in this play and nowhere else in the
plays of the Wakefield Master[12] is related also to the
theme of the duality of man. A contemporary manuscript connects the Trinity with the creation of man in
God's image: "Fferþermore, þat þou, lord, oon god
in þy now proved oonheed of beyng and of sub-
staunce has iij persoonys, euydence may be takun in
holy scripture, genesis jᵉ chapiter, where þou seidist
þus: 'Make we man to oure image and likenes.' lo, in
þis þat þou seidist, 'make we,' is meened þat mo
persoonys were þan oon which maden man, and ellis
woldis not haue seid, 'make we' for such speche in þe
plurel noumbre vndirstondun of oon persoon is
nouȝwhere ellis usid in holy scripture."[13] The mystery
of the Trinity emphasizes the double nature of man,
who, created in the likeness of his Creator, is completely different from him. The Trinity, a concept
unfathomable by natural reason,[14] forced man to contemplate the seemingly unspannable gap between the
human and the divine. The *Cursor mundi* provides a
homely comparison which explains how man may
bear the image of the Trinity, although no physical
trace of it can be found:

> Wherof mannes soule is wrouȝt
> Of goostly liȝt men say hit es
> þat god haþ made to his likenes
> As prent of seel in wax þrest
> þerynne he haþ his likenes fest.[15]

The importance of the Trinity as an organizing symbol for the play resides in the dual aspect of divinity's relation to man. The Trinity, a mysterious concept completely unlike man in essence, relates man to divinity in image. Noah, made in this image, must attempt to follow a divine pattern while remembering that as flesh he dwells in time.

The Wakefield Master captures the sense of being in the middle of time by condensing the span from the fall of Lucifer to Doomsday into the seven lines which precede the description of the making of man:

> He thoght hymself as worthi as hym that hym made,
> In brightnes, in bewty; therfor he hym degrade,
> Put hym in a low degre soyn after, in a brade,
> Hym and all his menye, where he may be vnglad
> For euer.
> Shall thay neuer wyn away
> Hence vnto domysday. (19–25)

By having Noah move rapidly along the chain of disobedience from Satan's fall, to Adam's fall, to the fallen state of men in his own age, the Wakefield Master creates the illusion that the present age as well as Noah's is threatened by the Flood.

The homiletic tone of Noah's evaluation of his own age would reinforce the audience's sense of contemporaneity:

> Bot now before his sight euery liffyng leyde,
> Most party day and nyght, syn in word and dede
> Full bold;
> Som in pride, ire, and enuy,
> Som in couetous and glotyny,
> Some in sloth and lechery,
> And other wise manyfold. (47–54)

This would remind the audience of some recent sermon condemning the present age.[16] Man as a compound of the Seven Deadly Sins seems to have lost his semblance of God. Noah reminds man of the mortal danger which threatens him when he forgets that he was made in the image of his maker.

The persistence of human sinfulness causes Noah to dwell on his mortality as it least resembles the infinite Trinity. He thinks of himself as little more than the lump of clay from which Adam was fashioned:

> Sex hundreth yeris and od haue I, without distance,
> In erth, as any sod, liffyd with grete grevance
> Allway. (57–59)

The span of six hundred years symbolizes human time from the fall until judgment day and further identifies Noah as mortal mankind.[17] The insistence throughout upon the "earthiness" of man (*homo* from *humus*) intensifies the feeling that human life is bounded by time and matter. In the play, man is clay, corrupt, and yet molded by a divine hand. The vision of man filling himself with corruption seems almost devoid of grace: "And now in grete reprufe full low ligys he, / In erth hymself to stuf with syn" (84–85). Isidore notes how man had originally been destined to rise from this abject state:

> For properly, *homo* from *humo*. The Greeks, however called man *anthropon,* because he could look upwards, raised up from the earth to contemplate his maker. The poet Ovid signifies this when he says:
>
>> Although the other beasts lay prone and gazed on the earth,
>> He gave man an uplifted face, and commanded him
>> To stand erect and turn his face to the stars.
>
> Man, therefore, erect, gazes on Heaven, so that he may seek God, and not turn toward the earth like the flocks that nature formed prone and obedient to the belly.[18]

The play's imagery evokes man as he is set forth in this pair of etymologies. In his prayer, Noah contemplates the created universe from the vastness of the heavens down to man set little lower than the angels, yet wretched in sinfulness. His view of mankind reaches a nadir when he looks at himself:

> And now I wax old,
> Seke, sory, and cold;
> As muk apon mold
> I widder away. (60–63)

For a moment, man seems no more than clay destined to return unlamented to the dust whence it sprang, but at this low point, Noah turns to God with the only boon requested in his long prayer, "bot yit will I cry for mercy and call" (64).

God does not answer the prayer directly, but does agree that man has reached his most worthless state:

> Methoght I shewed man luf when I made hym to be
> All angels abuf, like to the Trynyté;
> And now in grete reprufe full low ligys he. (82–84)

The arguments of justice precede those of mercy, so that for most of the speech it appears that man will not be saved. Noah had already reached the conclusion at which God seems to be aiming: "Therfor I drede lest God on vs will take veniance, / For syn is now alod, without any repentance" (55–56). This fearful speech ended with hope of mercy, but this seems dashed when Deus confirms Noah's conclusion: "Therfor shall I fordo all this medill-erd / With floodys that shall flo and ryn with hidous rerd" (100–101). When the audience hears Noah's own word "veniance" repeated and the destruction of all mankind threatened, "As I say shal I do—of veniance draw my swerd, / And make end / Of all that beris life" (103–5), they must concur with Noah that hope is at its lowest ebb. Noah's fears of total destruction seem realized, but just at this moment, God turns Noah's hope into promise, and with that promise, hope for all humanity:

> Sayf Noe and his wife,
> For thay wold neuer stryfe
> With me then me offend. (106–8)

The dramatic suspension of the word of Noah's protection gives the audience pause to reflect upon the nature of man and God's special relation to him. Among the analogues, the Wakefield play portrays the most distinct change from God the avenger to God the savior. In *Ludus Coventriae*, God puts an angel between himself and Noah, and in the York and Chester plays, Deus sends his orders for the ark from above. Only in the Wakefield play does God himself descend to tell Noah of his fate: "Hym to mekill wyn, hastly will I go / To Noe my seruand, or I blyn, to warn hym of his wo" (109–10). Noah's wonder at the appearance of God is the wonder of the psalmist who asks what man is that God visits him: "I thank the, Lord so dere, that wold vowchsayf / Thus low to appere to a symple knafe" (172–73).

IV

The argument between Noah and his wife that follows the appearance of God to Noah centers around two props, a prefabricated ark, that Noah constructs during the course of the play, and his wife's spinning wheel. Just how the ark is to be put together is not specified, but some inferences are possible about the staging of the scene and the nature of the performing area. As A. C. Cawley notes,[19] the fact that the *Mactacio Abel* calls for Cain to be driving what appears to be a real team requires that the ground level must be a playing area. In that play, the brothers go up a hill (170) to make their sacrifice, and then after the murder God speaks to Cain from a place above that. This indicates three levels of playing area: the ground, the stage on the pageant wagon with steps to the ground, and a balcony or upper stage on the wagon connected to the stage by steps or suspended by some kind of winch. In the first part of the Noah play, Noah is probably on the pageant stage so that God can come down to him in a single motion. Then when Noah says he must rush home (182), he would go down the steps to the ground level.

The staging of the *fabliau* part of the play depends upon the three-level playing area. Since it is unlikely, in those days before plywood, that one man could build a structure big enough to hold Noah's whole family (let us recall the struggle of the York carpenters with their crucifix), Noah probably uses the stage scaffolding for a frame upon which he places prefabricated pieces of an ark front. Going up on the ark, then, would mean going from the ground to the stage. Since Noah's wife remarks that her wheel is upon a hill, we are dealing with two raised loci, probably two ends of the pageant wagon which would be reached by going up steps. The similarity of Uxor's hill and the ark would make the building of the ark and her spinning parallel actions.

In the York play, the ark is already built when the fisticuffs begin a separate play, but at Wakefield the *fabliau* surrounds the ark-building. The audience is meant to wonder at the loss of dignity suffered by Noah as he is reduced from man's advocate to hen-pecked husband. This doubt will remain as the two go off to their respective loci, the place where the ark is being built and the hill with its spinning wheel. The focus is on Noah, but what is the wife doing all this while? Apparently sitting on her hill spinning, perhaps more and more furiously, as her husband finishes his work. She insists, after the ark is finished, that her work is as important as his.

In addition to establishing the parallel between the two kinds of busy-ness, the design of the ark could also suggest its allegorical values; a cross on the prow or even "stained glass" windows could suggest the ark as the church. Furthermore, since it is almost certain that the animals were represented by picture cards, they might well reinforce the thematic parallels of Noah's building of the ark and God's creation of the world. The Wakefield creation play does not have an elaborate seven-day creation like that in York, which was probably also done with cards representing the sun, the moon, the beasts, etc. It does, however, mention the creation of the beasts, which scene might well use the same or similar picture cards. If such cards were used in both places, the analogy of creation and ark-building would be made visually as well as verbally.

The marital conflict can be read as a way of dealing with the problems raised both about man's humanity and his likeness to God. Read figurally, the strife between Noah and his wife represents the relationship of God and man which led to the Fall and the Flood. At the same time, Noah's actions parody God's justice, displaying Noah's humanity at its most vulnerable. A costume change during the ark-building may emphasize this vulnerability. Noah removes his gown to work in his tunic, and with it he may be removing the last outward sign of the man who was fit to talk to God. The gown may be of the same style as the tunic or it may be the kind of garb usually used to designate members of the holy family. If the latter is the case, the audience would be shocked to discover that this man of stately appearance suddenly looks like one of their neighbors.

The statement that Noah was perfect in his generation meant that Noah was as good as one can expect of mankind: "If no one is without sin, how can anyone be perfect? Here some are called perfect, not like the saints when they are made perfect in that immortality in which they become equal to the angels of God, but as they can be perfect in this pilgrimage, where it significantly says; in his generation, to show that not according to the final justice, but according to the justice of his age he was just."[20] The playwright interprets this idea liberally to show the difficulties which true obedience can endure. Although Noah's attempts to impose order parody the divine wrath he has just witnessed, the burlesque does not invalidate the figural reading. Instead, it focuses on the type—Noah doing his best to fulfill his role as sovereign—to reveal the hardship and embarrassment encountered by man trying to act in the likeness of his maker. That this role is comic is to be expected when undertaken by a willing if imperfect man. The parody comes closer to its ideal when Noah turns his back on his wife's storming rage in an imitation of divine love and mercy:

> Thou can both byte and whyne
> With a rerd; . . .
> Bot I will kepe charyté, for I haue at do.
>
> (229–230, 235)

To link cosmic and human sovereignty, the playwright likens the relationship between God and man to that between man and wife. The voice of Deus is like that of a forsaken husband when he reminds man that love, which should be mutual, has gone only one way:

Man must luf me paramoure . . .
Me thoght I shewed man luf when I made hym to be
All angels abuf, like to the Trynyté. (80, 82–83)

God mourns man's degeneration from his state of
grace, "farest of favoure," as would a husband whose
wife had deceived him.

In an ideal marriage, the husband must esteem his
wife as he does himself, but this does not mean a
change of order: "Netheles and ȝe alle, ech man loue
his wyf as him silf; forsoth the wyf drede hir hose-
bonde" (Eph. 5:33). Furthermore, woman should be
completely obedient to her husband. Deus requires
the same of man: "Euery man to my bydyng shuld be
bowand / Full feruent" (76–77). Paul urges this attitude, a reflection of man's submission to the Lord,
upon all wives: "Wymmen, be thei suget to her hose-
bondis, as to the Lord" (Eph. 5:22). This, in turn,
derives from the injunction to Eve after the Fall:

> And þou wommon for þis dere . . .
> þou shal be vndir mannes hest
> To hem be buxom meest & leest.[21]

Any woman, like the Wife of Bath, who desires sovereignty, disregards the half of the Pauline admonition
that stresses mutual love.[22] In the Wakefield play,
Deus complains that man has come to regard him as
Noah's wife does her husband: "Bi me he settys no
store, and I am his soferan" (92). Disobedience has
become man's way of life.

The figural reading of the play rests upon the chain
of disobedience described in Noah's prayer and represented by Uxor's behavior. The emphasis on the upset
of degree is unmatched in the other English versions.
The Chester analogue does not connect the Fall with
the Flood; the Chester audience knows only that because man has fallen into sin he must be destroyed.

The York playwright alludes to Adam and Eve, but does not link them to the flood. The connection of Noah with Adam, which Chambers[23] feels is missing from the Wakefield play, is found only in the *Ludus Coventriae:*

> In me Noe, þe secunde age
> indede be-gynnyth, as I ȝou say
> afftyr Adam, with-outyn langage
> þe secunde fadyr am I in fay.[24]

This play, however, makes Lamech's slaying of Cain the immediate cause of the flood and does not connect the disobedience of Adam and Eve to man's disobedience before the deluge. Furthermore, in the *Ludus Coventriae,* Noah's wife follows the French model and is no shrew.[25]

The Wakefield Master, on the other hand, ties together the disobedience in Eden, the disobedience of mankind before the flood, and the rebellious behavior of Noah's wife. Uxor's violation of her husband's sovereignty is analogized to Eve's and symbolizes mankind's fractiousness toward God.[26] As ark-builder Noah becomes a creator and his trouble in getting his wife aboard parallels the difficulties which the Creator has had in placing man in his creation.[27]

Although the relationship between Noah and his wife is at all times comic, the playwright recognizes the potential evil in her disobedience. More than a loud, stubborn woman, she is malicious as well:

> What with gam and with gyle,
> I shall smyte and smyle,
> And qwite hym his mede. (214–16)

Uxor's wish for Noah's death, "Lord, I were at ese, and hertely full hoylle, / Might I onys haue a measse of wedows coyll" (388–89), said in soliloquy rather than as excited rejoinder, exceeds the limits of shrew-

ishness. Uxor's complaints about her husband surpass
those of the wives in the other cycles.[28]

In both the Chester and the York plays, the wives
are stubborn and garrulous, but not vicious. Both refuse to leave their gossips—a somewhat valid reason
for not entering the ship. The Chester playwright
places the gossips on stage, entreating for mercy,
which mitigates the wife's wilfulness. Although she
eventually relents, her reluctance is understandable
because she is using herself as a pawn to save her
friends. Her attempt to force the will of God towards
mercy parallels her husband's similar, although less
strong-willed, attempt to ward off divine judgment:[29]

> A 100 wynters and 20
> this shipp making taried haue I,
> if through amendment any mercye
> wolde fall vnto mankind.[30]

No similar excuse is given the Wakefield wife. Instead, she is linked with Eve by her husband as the
"begynnar of blunder" (406). The spinning supports
this parallel, since this was popularly conceived of as
Eve's occupation after the Fall: "Now bithenk thee,
gentilman, / How Adam dalf and Eve span."[31] The
Wakefield Uxor is closest to the Newcastle version:
"On analogy with the Adam and Eve story, the devil
is introduced to tempt *uxor* to make trouble for
Noah."[32]

While concern for her neighbors motivates Noah's
wife in Chester and York, Uxor's spinning is her excuse for not entering the ark. By replacing the fear for
the life of the gossips with the concern about her spinning, the Wakefield dramatist makes Noah's wife one
of those characters in his plays who is more concerned
with the things of the world than with salvation.
Noah's remark, "Ther is garn on the reyll other"

(298), reminds us of the two classes of enterprise at hand: the business of salvation and the business of existing on this earth. Noah's wife is concerned only with the latter. Her first greeting to her husband connects her with Eve, whose sin, according to Noah (37), was gluttony:

> When we swete or swynk,
> Thou dos what thou thynk,
> Yit of mete and of drynk
> Haue we veray skant. (195–98)

The audience would be expected to sympathize with the wife's worry about having enough to eat, but it must also realize that man's purpose on earth is not to feed only his body.

Uxor's concern with wordly goods is symbolized when she releases the raven after the flood. In the Bible and in the other English plays, Noah releases both raven and dove. Here the raven shares the characteristics of Noah's wife:

> The ravyn is a-hungrye
> Allway.
> He is without any reson;
> And he fynd any caryon,
>
> ....
>
> He will not away. (499–504)

The raven was connected with carnality and its lack of reason parallels Uxor's wilfulness: "The Scripture says, 'The raven did not return to the ark,' perhaps because it was cut off by the flood waters and perished or perhaps it perched upon some cadaver that it found. Similarly, the sinner who feeds on fleshly desires, like the crow who did not return to the ark, is detained by surface considerations."[33]

Noah vainly tries to tell his wife of the purpose of

life beyond her petty interests: "Wife we are hard sted with tythyngys new" (199). In the York play, on the other hand, Noah's wife is very upset because her husband has not told her of the dangers to be faced by them both. Her reaction makes the York wife quite appealing, since the slight she feels shows her concern with her family, not herself.

Only in the Wakefield play does the wife repeat her disobedience after she has entered the ark. Her new reason for refusing, simple wilful defiance—"I will not, for thi bydyng" (375)—recalls God's complaint about man: "Every man to my bydyng shuld be bowand" (76). Uxor's tone indicates that her challenge is motivated by unalloyed audacity: "Spare me not, I pray the, bot euen as thou thynk; / Thise grete wordys shall not flay me" (379–80). God had already complained of the same kind of boldness in man: "For me no man is ferd" (102). When his wife refuses to obey him, Noah knows that he must chastise her a second time as God has twice chastised man, first with the expulsion from the Garden and then with the Flood.

The tone in which Uxor refuses to enter the ark characterizes, in the playwright's own time, the rebellious humanity who cannot understand how close they are to the Judgment. The urgency of Noah's response depends upon the typology of the Flood as Judgment Day. A sermon of Augustine's tells us to prepare for the day of Doom by entering the ark of the Church now: "For, although sinners ourselves, we announce to you in imitation of Saint Noah the coming destruction of the world; and we say that they only will avoid the danger, whom the threefold ark encloses within its bosom. For the threefold ark is the Church because it contains the sacrament of the Trinity. . . . We therefore announce, like Noah, the coming wreck of the

world, and we urge all men into this house."[34] Langland also sees the flood as a warning to sinners (here
specifically clerics) to remember the last day:

At domes day a dyluuye worth • of deth and fuyr at ones;
Worcheth, ʒe wryghtes of holichurche • as holy writ
    techeth
Lest ʒe be lost as the laborers were • that labored vnder
    noe.[35]

These laborers scoffed at Noah as a gloomy eccentric
in much the way Noah's wife does in the Wakefield
play.

Kolve explains that biblical time was related to the
English present in a way which would remind the audience that they were still in the time when grace was
not put away. " 'Now' is the time of grace and in so
recognizing it the medieval cycle drama makes its only
direct address to the present moment. Such a recognition was necessary because the duration of grace was
limited—it could end at any moment for any man, as
for all men at doomsday."[36] Such a conception humanizes the obdurateness of Noah's wife by including it
with the audience's similar failings.

Uxor reacts to Noah's warnings as a stubborn pa-
rishioner would respond to an austere sermon on the
approach of the End. She continually accuses Noah of
being too pessimistic:

For thou art always adred, be it fals or trew . . .
Thou spekys euer of sorow;
God send the onys thi fill. (201, 206–7)

What Uxor protests against is Noah's sober Christian
attitude, which always considers the Last Day and consequently must be full of dread. A thirteenth-century
lyric on the Judgment summarizes this attitude:
"Wenne hi þenche on domes-dai ful sore i me adrede. /
þer scal after his werec huc mon fongon mede."[37]

Uxor's eagerness not to believe in the flood gives an optative quality to her refusal; that is, by not believing she unconsciously hopes that she can avert the deluge. This approach has provided false comfort in all generations: Ignore the crisis and maybe it will go away. Such a state of mind explains Uxor's frantic calm—her urgent insistence on business as usual. Through the completion of her spinning even as the rains begin to fall, she hopes to convince herself and perhaps the universe that everything is normal. This interpretation of the wife's behavior allows us to see the sympathy in the playwright's view of her. He has humanized her typological role as initiator of discord by making her do the "reasonable" thing in the face of an incomprehensible Judgment. This aspect of the playwright's art would be explained away by a strictly figural analysis.

V

While the disobedience of Uxor has been developing, a parallel action reminds the audience of the proper way to conduct life in relation to both God and spouse. Noah's building of the ark most clearly represents this attitude. His work, unlike his wife's spinning, is not just a way to fill the time. He is an old man and the work is hard and hot. Although he acts in obedience and knows that his effort is entirely due to a strength not his own—"Hym that maide all of noght / I thank oonly" (287–88)[38]—he is not relieved from effort, as is his York counterpart:

> Fyfe hundreth wyntres I am of elde,
> Me thynk þer ʒeris as yestirday.
> Ful wayke I was and all vnwelde,
> My weryness is wente away.[39]

Noah's sons' obedience "without any yelp" further exemplifies the proper way to behave toward the orders
of a sovereign.

The building of the ark is a metaphor for salvation
which can come only through obedience. The effect of
obedience is brought out in the change which comes
over the family once the fighting stops; disobedience
and discord end together. The blessing that Noah had
requested, "Blis us Lord . . . / the better may we stere
the ship that we shall have" (174–75), marks the first
act of obedience which governs the Noah family. Once
the proper hierarchy has been established, Noah can
entrust the steering of the ship to his wife, since she
will, through him, be ruled by God, "the stere-man
good" (428):[40]

> NOE: Wife, tent the stere-tre, and I shall asay
>   The depness of the see that we bere, if I may.
> UXOR: That shall I do ful wysely. (433–35)

Now they are ready to "wax and multiply / and fill
the erth agane" (179–80). Their state contrasts with
that of Adam and Eve, who failed to "multiplie without discord" (31). The playwright emphasizes the
achievement of concord by a pun upon the name of
the country in which they land. In answer to his
wife's question, Noah indicates a spiritual state as
well as a geographical place:

> UXOR: Then begynnys to grufe to vs mery chere.
>   Bot, husband,
>   What grownd may this be?
> NOE: The hyllys of Armonye. (463–66)

The Wakefield Master did not invent this place of
landing (the Vulgate has the country, not the moun-
tain, Ararat),[41] but he exploits it to make the point
that there can be no harmony without obedience. He

shows the truth of this in the relation of man to God as well as wife to husband.

The operation of parody allows the audience to identify with this family, in which domestic hierarchy and a sense of community welfare have been reestablished. The separate occupations of husband and wife merge into common profit which accords with Ambrose's understanding of the story: "Many men are disturbed because the scripture does not say that the Lord was mindful also of Noah's wife and children. . . . But when it says he was mindful of Noah it understands in the father and head of the household the other relatives as well. . . . For where all are mutually beloved, the house is one; but when they disagree, they are separated and split into several houses. Where charity exists, therefore, there the name of the elder belongs to the others, which signifies the whole house."[42] The unity of Noah's household is symbolized by the wife's movement, not merely onto the ark, but from the wheel to the tiller. If both props are given equal prominence and perhaps placed at symmetric points on the pageant stage, the wife's new role would be emphasized.

The vision which sees Noah's task as both a type of the creation and also a fragile parody of it suggests to the listeners that God will be mindful of them if they fare as well in their imitation of the Creator. Each member of the audience is urged to expand and contract his vision, to let his eye encompass the great scheme which has ordered all history and the fate of the race, while still noticing his likeness to the very contemporary figures who stand before him adumbrating his own weakness and his own promise. Auerbach's understanding of Adam and Eve in the French mystery play applies to Noah and his wife as well: "The scenes which render everyday contemporary

life . . . are, then, fitted into a Biblical and world historical frame by whose spirit they are pervaded. This
implies that every occurrence, in all its every day reality, is simultaneously a part of the world-historical
context through which each part is related to every
other and thus is likewise regarded as being of all
times or above time."[43] The figural reading of the play
intensifies the sense that each act performed by man
occurs in time yet resonates beyond it. The playwright
responds like the psalmist to the paradoxical nature of
man and understands that God is mindful of man
when he seems least so and that despite his wrath, he
patiently awaits man's mutual remembrance of him.

IV · *Prima pastorum*

FOLLY HUNGERS AFTER THE NEW WISDOM

Although many of the plays of the Wakefield Master are experiments in the creation of multiple mirror images through allegory and parody, the *Prima pastorum* examines the growth of the imagination as it learns how to read symbolic meanings. The playwright does not forsake allegory and parody in this play, but his primary interest is in the process of interpreting rather than in the meaning itself. For the playwright, only the man possessing a symbolic imagination can perceive the spiritual meaning of the things of this world. Although the final vision is a gift, the imaginative faculty must be developed properly to perceive it. In the *Prima pastorum,* three unlikely protagonists show how the symbolic imagination is acquired. The three foolish shepherds can become prophets of Christ only when they leave off their literal ways and learn to view the world imaginatively. This process of transition from the literal to the symbolic requires several steps, and the action of the play follows the successive stages in this radical change in perception.

The play culminates in the Nativity, but the bulk of the action is devoted to watching the shepherds expand their imaginations so that they can comprehend the vision when it is sent to them. As the play opens, the shepherds are prevented from perceiving Truth because of their concern with the unstable world of time. They must move from this profane world to the new order of time (the *nova progenies* of Vergil's Messianic Eclogue, cited in the play) that begins with the Nativity. The playwright demonstrates the steps of this process, first, by using their complaints to present iconographically the fallen world of time, and then by showing how this image of the world is transformed successively into worlds imagined by emotional need, by aesthetic appreciation, and finally by spiritual insight. When the shepherds reach the final stage they are ready to perceive the Nativity.

The play opens with a description of the unstable world that merges the dual roles of the protagonists; they are both biblical shepherds living in the pre-Nativity world and fifteenth-century shepherds suffering from the hardships of the English countryside. The contemporary English scene is appropriate to the biblical one because the cold, barren English winter represents man's world before the advent of Christ, whether physically in the first century or spiritually in the fifteenth. The dismaying change of seasons, which nearly overwhelms the first shepherd, symbolizes the mutability of "this world here":

> Now in hart, now in heyll, now in weytt, now in blast;
> Now in care,
> Now in comforth agane;
> Now in fayre, now in rane, . . .
> And after full sare.
> Thus this warld, as I say, farys on ylk syde. (4–10)

Richard Rolle states explicitly what the playwright presents symbolically:

> And for-þi þat þe worlde is swa unstable,
> Alle þat men sese þar-in es chaungeable;
> For God ordayns here, al es his wille,
> Sere variaunce, for certayn skille,
> Of the tyms and wedirs and sesons

> In taken of þe worldes condicion,
> þat swa unstable er and variande.[1]

Rolle goes on to suggest, as the playwright will, that the only way to deal satisfactorily with this world is to see beyond it.

As the play opens, the first shepherd does not have the wisdom to see beyond the world as the Fall left it. The Fall, as Rolle tells us, separated the mutable sublunary world of man from the changeless sphere of Heaven, creating two worlds:

> For a grete clerk says, þat hight Berthelmewe,
> þat twa worldes er principaly to shewe. . . .
> þe tan es gastly, invisile and clene,
> þe toþer es bodyly and may be sene.[2]

At the manger the shepherds will see the borders of this invisible world, but first they must come to terms with the world which the Fall has involved in profane time.

After presenting a list containing some fifty "now's," which, like the shepherd's shorter list, illustrates the changing conditions of this world, Rolle states the folly of mundane concerns "for the world til the endeward fast draws." Although the shepherd in the Wakefield play is right when he complains, "Thus this warld, as I say, farys on ylk syde," he has yet to learn the limited importance of statements about this world. It is appropriate that this shepherd, so concerned at first with the here and now, will later speak of a "new kinde" when he translates two lines from the Messianic Eclogue.

The lines from the eclogue also help explain the function of the second shepherd's complaint about the "gentlery" men as a further depiction of the unstable world. The presence of these men, who seem greater than their masters, is symbolic of the inversion of order that accompanies the end of Saturn's first reign.

The departure of the maiden Astrea began the reign of injustice in which the second shepherd finds himself, but the end of this violation of order is also promised by the end of the eclogue: "Iam rediet Virgo redeunt Saturnia regna" (388).

Once the complaints establish the shepherds' initial image of the world, the playwright examines the way in which his heroes gradually reconstruct this image. A lyric in the Vernon manuscript, which uses a list of "now's" like that in the Wakefield play, calls for a wise man to explain the mutable world:

> I wolde witen of sum wys wiht
> Witterly what þis world were. . . .
> Now is hit henne, now is hit here:
> Ne be we neuer so much of miht,
> Now be we on benche, now be we on bere.[3]

The first comic action of the play, the fight over imaginary sheep, is taken from a story in which the protagonists are ironically called the Wise Men of Gotham. The playwright will eventually defuse the irony of this designation so that his heroes do, in fact, provide the wisdom sought in the Vernon lyric.

By the time the tale reached the sixteenth century, and probably in the playwright's time as well, it had acquired a moral about the relation of folly to wisdom:[4] "Thys tale shewyth you, that som man takyth upon hym for to teche other men wysdome, when he is but a fole hymselfe."[5] When the play closes, it will be shown that a fool can indeed teach other men wisdom.

The fact that the play constitutes an attempt to right the world by the application of wisdom is first hinted at by the first shepherd, who vows "by my wytt to fynde to cast the warld in seuen" (38). At this point "wytt" simply means native intelligence, but the word will mean wisdom by the end of the play. Although the phrase for turning the world over to chance is usually "at sixes and sevens,"[6] the Wakefield Master chooses this particular expression to underscore the fact that chance does not ultimately rule: Christ also "cast the warld in seuen"—seven days.[7] The shepherds' still barren "wytt" cannot yet "fynde" any implication beyond chance in the phrase "cast the warld in seuen." When the shepherds are no longer "bare of wysdom to know" (161), however, Mary will echo this phrase to remind them that nothing is ever turned over to chance: "The makere of heuen . . . / Rewarde you this day, as he sett all on seuen" (485–87).

II

The shepherds' first attempt to reconstruct the image of the world—in the quarrel over imaginary sheep—is prefaced by the proverbial remark "first must vs crepe and sythen go" (100). This applies not only to their attempt to increase their income, but also to the development of "wytt," which also requires man to crawl before he can walk. The argument over the "sheep" is the first stage in the development of the symbolic imagination.

In the narrative versions of the Three Wise Men of Gotham the quarrel has no context and is presented merely as folly, but with the shepherds' desperate complaints in the background, the conjuring up of the sheep meets an emotional need. The first shepherd's imagination not only undoes the ravages of the rot, it can also temporarily suspend the terrifying winter and replace it with a landscape that has greenery for his visionary flock:

> I wyll pasture my fe
> Wheresoeuer lykys me;
> Here shall thou theym se. (105–7)

At this point the shepherds have started to use their imaginative faculty, but its use is completely literal; they simply objectify their wishes. There are, however, two fragments in the Fools of Gotham episode which point toward the Pauline notion of things seen and not seen: "Vs not biholdynge tho thingis that ben seyn, but tho that ben not seyn. Sothli tho thingis that be seyn, ben temperal, *or durynge by short tyme;* forsothe tho thingis that ben not seyn, ben everlastinge *or withouten ende*" (2 Cor. 4:18).[8] Both the reference to the milkmaid Mowll and the appearance of Garcio to remind the shepherds of the excellent health of their nonexistent sheep hint at a significance which transcends the literal imagination.

The entrance of the third shepherd prepares for Garcio's appearance. He asks a question which seems a cruel reminder of the first shepherd's plight: "Ye bot tell me, good, wher ar youre shepe, lo?" (135). When the first shepherd makes no answer, the second shepherd replies that his companion has had no sheep as long as they have been standing there. The audience has already heard that he once had sheep:

> All my shepe ar gone,
> I am not left oone,
> The rott has theym slone. (24–26)

The importance of the rot in the fifteenth century[9] would make it impossible for the audience to forget the diseased flock when Garcio appears. With this in mind, Garcio's reponse to the first shepherd's question, "How pastures our fee?" (100) is expected to shock the audience. Instead of reminding him that his sheep are dead and rotten, Garcio replies that his stock is thriving miraculously in the dead of winter: "Thay are gryssed to the kne" (189). Cawley points out that this unseasonable occurrence "can be taken as a symbol of midwinter fertility, a parallel to the miraculous birth of Christ."[10] This change in landscape parallels a legend found in the *Cursor mundi* and the *South English Legendary*, that barrenness accompanied the coming of sin and that only with the coming of Christ will verdure be restored.[11] The return of greenness, then, occurs in sacred rather than profane time. When the shepherd fully understands the implications of Garcio's answer, the end of spiritual winter is at hand.

Garcio's brief appearance needs some study. His name suggests that he is the mischievous boy of many of the plays, like Pikeharnys in *Mactacio Abel* or Froward in *Coliphizacio*. The boy's typical role is that of deflater of swollen egos, and he is as close to a skeptic as one can find in the plays. Jack Garcio fulfills the audience's expectations when he undermines the shepherds' talk of wisdom by identifying them as the Fools of Gotham:

> Now God gyf you care, foles all sam!
> Sagh I neuer none so fare bot the foles of Gotham.
>
> ....
>
> Of all the foles I can tell.
> From heuen vnto hell,
> Ye thre bere the bell. (179–80, 184–86)

His first function then is to show that they are wise men without wisdom, just as they are shepherds without sheep.

Still this rather obvious conclusion hardly justifies the introduction of a new character who speaks only a few more lines before disappearing, never to be heard from again. As a skeptical realist, Garcio is necessary because his realism gives his brief announcement of a miracle the weight of reality. If one of the shepherds had responded, "They are gryssed to the kne," the audience would take it as part of the fanciful argument about the imaginary sheep. Garcio, then, has a number of roles. He is a choric figure who identifies the shepherds as the "Wise Men" of Gotham, a skeptic who reports a miracle, and finally, the one who points out to the shepherds the only way to see the miracle: "If ye will ye may se; youre bestes ye ken" (190).

The theme of incorruptible sheep is implicit in the brief reference to Mowll, the milkmaid. The allusion, ostensibly to illustrate the proverb about not counting your chickens before they hatch—"it is far to byd 'hyte' / To an eg or it go" (150–51)—has a second thematic application. The story, of ancient folk origins, tells of a milkmaid who, on her way to market, reflects how she will sell her milk, buy a hen, raise chickens, sell them to buy a pig, fatten and sell it, and buy a foal. When the colt is grown she will ride it and say, "Io! io!" While daydreaming about her future wealth, she claps her hands in joy and breaks the pitcher of milk. The Wakefield account differs from the many extant versions of the tale in one significant respect: In all the other tales, when the milkmaid breaks her pitcher she has nothing left.[12] Here, and we are reminded of it twice, one sheep remains to her: "Many shepe can she poll, bot oone had she ay . . . / Bot oone shepe yit she hade" (154, 158). The sheep she is going to buy and shear are illusory. Nevertheless, unlike the first shepherd, who claims that he has no sheep left, Mowll still has one sheep even after "hyr . . . pycher . . . was broken" (155–56). In the context of this play, in which "to the lawde of this lam, / syng we in syght" (501–2), there can be no question that this sheep refers to Christ.

"The skarthis," the third shepherd remarks, "was the tokyn" (160). The fragments betoken not merely the broken pitcher but all the fragile wordly things upon which one depends. In spite of the shards, Mowll had no reason to despair, since "oone had she ay." The tale comments on the shepherds' quarrel by showing that in creating illusory sheep they have ignored the Lamb of God, and so have no "helpars" in their misfortune.

Understanding the tale of Mowll or Garcio's remark requires a kind of "witt" (imaginative wisdom) which the shepherds have not yet acquired. The playwright borrows from the popular literature of his age a pregnant, albeit naïve, notion about the relation of the literal to the symbolic. He then refines it in the comic action of the play. A tale from a jest book which includes the story of the Three Wise Men of Gotham provides the germ for the Wakefield Master's development of the Mowll episode.

The tale shows how the literalizing imagination can take a spiritual concept and convert it to worldly logic. The story concerns "a certayne confessour, [who] in the holy tyme of Lente, enioyned his penytente to saye dayly for his penaunce this prayer: Agnus dei miserere mei."[13] The penitent returns after a year and holds the following dialogue with his confessor: "I haue sayd thus to day mornynge and so dayly: the shepe of God haue mercy vpon me. To whome the confessour said: nay, I bad the say: Agnus Dei miserere mei, that is, the Lamb of God haue mercy vpon me. Ye, syr, quod the penytente, ye say truthe; that was the laste yere. But now it is at twelfemonthe since, and it is a shepe by this tyme."[14] The moral to the story denies the penitent's imaginative transformation of a stock symbolic sign: "By this tale ye may perceyue, that if holy scripture be expownyd to the lay people onely in the lytterall sence, peraduenture it shall do lytell good."[15]

The Wakefield playwright's approach to symbolism is more fluid than that of the writer of the tale, because he has combined the logic of both confessor and penitent. In his play the spiritual understanding of the confessor is grafted onto the realistic imagination of the penitent. The playwright will, like the penitent, allow a Lamb to grow into a sheep (or vice versa), but like the confessor he always keeps its spiritual value in mind. If, for example, wisdom nourishes the soul, his characters, by the penitent's logic, will literally try to chew and swallow it; but by the confessor's logic, they may be sustained by the feast of wisdom. From this double point of view the transition from Mowll's sheep to the Lamb of God is possible. Later in the cycle an actual lamb is a prop, when Jesus gives the *agnus Dei* to John the Baptist.[16]

During their quarrel the shepherds' perceptions pass through their minds unchanged: "And ye look well abowte, nawther more nor myn; / So gose your wyttys owte, evyn as it com in" (173–74). The third shepherd reverses the imaginative process of the first two by turning things into words through his expensive metaphor, but in both cases the shepherds are literalists of the imagination. Unable to glean any symbolic import from the tale of Mowll and her eternal sheep, they can only make a narrow transition from words to things. They have none of the insight they will later display in discerning Mary's virginity in the burning bush:

> 3 Pastor: Of hym spake Ieromy, and Moyses also,
>   Where he sagh hym by a bushe burnand, lo!
>   When he cam to aspy if it were so,
>   Vnburnyd was it truly at commyng therto—
>   A wonder!
> I Pastor: That was for to se
>   Hir holy vyrgynyté. (359–65)

Such interpretation requires amplification of the original perception: the burning bush is to be seen as more than a bush that burns.

The third shepherd, who, by emptying his sack of wheat joins these other two fools, does not merely remind them of the loss of their wits; he also urges them to seek their wits again: "Geder vp / And seke it agane!" (174–75). The second shepherd recognizes the point of this admonition and decides to go with his fellows "wydsom to sup" (178). This advice and the ironically self-mocking comment, "it is wonder to wyt where wytt shuld be fownde" (143), suggests the beginning of a search for a new kind, rather than merely a new store, of wisdom. The remark not only looks back to the foolishness which has been witnessed, but also forward to the wondrous display of religious "wytt" on the part of the shepherds when they review the prophetic foreshadowings of the Nativity. The shepherds, now worldly fools, will become fools for Christ.

III

"Wysdom to sup." The words mean little to the shepherds, but they combine mysteriously with Garcio's allusion to midwinter verdure as a prologue to the shepherds' feast. The shepherds do not go immediately to taste "wysdom," but rather to fill their bellies. Their dinner is a parody of the Christmas feast, filled with misplaced allusions to the Nativity. When the third shepherd remarks, "My seruyse I tyne; I fare full yll / At youre mangere" (201–2), he is unaware of the ironic contrast with worship at Christ's manger. "Let vs cryb furst" (208) also recalls the manger and states the proper goal.

As the banquet begins, the shepherds joke about using knowledge to stave off hunger. The third shepherd mocks his companion—"Cowth ye by youre gramery reche vs a drynk, / I shuld be more mery" (242–43)—but, for the Middle Ages, wisdom could sate man's inner hunger: "þe ʒifte of wisdom . . . þe Holi Gost ʒeueþ hym þat he knytteþ hym to God bi a swete swolewyng of loue, so þat he is al on wiþ God; þer he fedeþ hymself, þer he norescheþ hymself, þer he wexeþ in good poynt, . . . þer he forʒeteþ al his trauaile, alle his desires of þe flesch and of þe world."[17] With this in mind, it is not surprising that "by grameré" is repeated to introduce the Messianic Eclogue when the shepherds achieve spiritual wisdom.

As long as the Christmas feast retains the spirit of gluttony, fighting, and blasphemy, no one can be fed. Paul warns that Communion, which is the paradigm of this feast, depends upon the worthiness of the communicants: "For he that etith and drinkith vnworthili, etith and drinkith doom to hym, not wiseli demyng the body of the Lord. . . . Therfor, my britheren, whan ʒe comen togidere to ete, abide ʒe toʒidere" (1 Cor. 11: 29, 33). Since the shepherds eat and drink unworthily, they fail to perceive the Lord. The first shepherd addresses the bottle with words fit for Christ: "This is boyte of our bayll, / Good holsom ayll" (247–48). Noah, in the *Processus,* properly calls God, "beytter of bayll."[18]

The "grotesque" Christmas banquet marks a turning point in the creative vision of the shepherds. The feast stands midway between the literalizing imagination of the Wise Men of Gotham scene and the symbolic understanding displayed by the prophetic shepherds. Cawley notes an imaginative mind at work in this scene, but ascribes it to the wrong source: "The playwright's mixing of high-class and low-class table delicacies makes a ludicrous gallimaufry that can never have existed except in his imagination."[19] The playwright, rather, wishes to show the shepherds' imagination at work creating this feast. The shepherds' creative approach is seen in the apostrophe to the cup, "Be thou wyne, be thou ayll, / Bot if my brethe fayll, / I shall set the on sayll" (256–58), which, in the context of an imaginary feast, is a fiat rather than an expression of doubt about its contents.

The conjuring up of drink is closely related to a tradition about imbibing wisdom which contrasts man's depressing weakness of wit with the inebriated joy of wisdom. *The Book of Vices and Virtues* suggests what a man with spiritual imagination might find in the bottle:

> þerfore þe grete swetnesse þat þe contemplatif herte haþ and feleþ bi þe ȝifte of wisdom in þis dedli lif nys but a litle taste wher-by men han sauour and felen how God is swete and softe, and who-so tasteþ þe sauour of þe wyne er men drynken þer-of a ful drauȝt; but þei schulle see & come to þat gret tauerne where þat þe tunne is made al comune, þᵗ is in the life wiþouten ende, where þe wyne of loue, of pees, and of ioie and solas schal be ȝeue so largeliche to euery wiȝt þat comeþ þider þat all schul be fulfilled, as þe Sauter seiþ, þat al þe desire of þe herte schal be fulfilled whan God schal make aliȝt vpon his frendes a streme of pees, as þe prophete seiþ, wher-wiþ þei schulle be alle as drunken.[20]

The homely image of Heaven as a great tavern where the cup of wisdom goes round would fit the style of the Wakefield Master, who also envisions spiritual ideals in humble symbolic referents.

Margery Morgan points out how the dramatist uses allusion to place the meal formally in the play's structure: "The episodes of the grotesque meal and the shepherds' recollection of the messianic prophecies are brought into formal relation (catalogs of physical and spiritual food) by the conclusion of both with passages that turn on the same key words."[21] What has not been noticed is that the scene shows the shepherds in the process of developing a more fertile imagination, which will ultimately enable them to interpret the Messianic prophecies. Cawley has pointed out the richness of the meal described by the third shepherd, but he ascribes this to greater knowledge rather than greater imagination: "Although the other shepherds have a nodding acquaintance with the aristocratic menus of their day, it is clear the third shepherd impressed them both with his culinary learning."[22] The meal begins fit for a glutton and progresses imaginatively until it is suitable for a gourmet. The change is from the physical and corruptible, if not yet to the spiritual, at least to the aesthetic. The third shepherd has managed an aesthetic restoration ("restorité") of "moton of an ewe that was roton" (220–21), transforming it into a meal fit for a lord. The shepherds have not yet reached the point where they understand that Christ is the only true healer of rot, both physical and spiritual. This they will learn at the close of the play: "We mon all be restorde—God graunt it be so!" (496).

Although the scene makes perfect sense if it is read according to the theory (of Cawley and Morgan) that it is conducted in mime, this involves some awkwardness at the end, when the shepherds charitably decide to give their meal to the poor. To make that part of the scene work, it is more likely that the shepherds have before them as simple a meal as possible, probably bread and ale, which they imaginatively convert into a gourmet dinner. An Advent carol (c. 1492) parallels the contrast in the scene. Apparently "Advent was sometimes actually impersonated as we know Christmas and Lent to have been."[23] In the carol, the speaker complains about the penitential fare that the personified Advent brings, and looks forward to the return of Christmas cheer:

> Farewele, Aduent; Cristemas is cum;
> Farewele fro vs both alle and sume.
>
> ....
>
> While thou haste be within oure howse
> We ete no puddynges ne no sowce,
> But stynking fisshe not worthe a lowce.
>
> ....
>
> Oure brede was browne, oure ale was thynne,
> Oure brede was musty in the bynne,
> Oure ale soure or we did begynne.[24]

The poet's querulous description of Advent awaits the rich Christmas feasting described in the boar's head carols which are as likely a source as any for the shepherds' menu.[25] While the scene would be comic in mime, it would be equally funny as the shepherds turn into gourmets over a plain loaf of bread.

The final mouthwatering description of the feast is meant to entice the audience as well as the other shepherds, for the play must show how easily worldly sustenance slips from one's grasp. When the first shepherd breaks up his companion's description with a caustic "yee speke all by clergé" (240), both the audience and the shepherds feel that the meal, which seemed so real a moment before, never existed. Approaching wisdom without grasping it is like seeing wine in a glass without being able to taste it: "But þe ʒifte of wisdom is non oþer þing þan a sauerous knowynge, þat is a good sauour and a grete delite in þe herte. For oþer-wise knoweþ he þe wyn þat seeþ it in a faire pece or verre, and oþer-wise he þat tasteþ it, drynkeþ it, and sauoureþ it."[26] The description of the feast that never appears is to contrast with the prophecy of the Nativity, which is then embodied on stage.

At the height of his description, the third shepherd can cure rotten sheep through the aesthetic use of the imagination, but the play ultimately shows that Christ is the only restorative helpful to man.[27] Nevertheless, the aesthetic imagination is only a step away from the imaginative appreciation of spiritual phenomena as it is stressed by Lydgate. Lydgate urges man to make the leap from manna to grace in order to understand the symbolic value of Communion:

> So as Manna was a Restauratyf
> To chyldren of Israel, gayne bodyly trauayle,
> Let vs well trust in our ymagynatyf,
> How moche the syght may helpen and preuayle
> Of the sacrament impossybyll for to fayle.[28]

Richard Rolle also realizes that man cannot conceive of the heavenly city unless vision makes the invisible world visible. To fill the gap temporarily, he relies on imagination, which for him is midway between earthly and spiritual knowledge:

> Na man wate properly how it es made,
> Ne can, thurgh wrytt, ymagyn in thoght
> of whatkyn matere it es wroght. . . .
> Bot alle-if I kan noght descryve þat stede,
> yhit will I ymagyn, on myne awen hede,
> Ffor to gyf it a descripcion.[29]

The imagination which can turn a shepherd's meal into a regal banquet is developing until it can discern the King of Kings when he is born in a manger. A contemporary lyric tells us that the great wonder "to monnus witte" was that royalty had chosen such poverty for its birthplace:

> to monnus witte wonder hit was
> that he that was of miȝtes most
> Wold light into so pore a place.[30]

The literalists of "mannish wit," like those in Herod's court, would find the conjunction of king and stable absurd. Imagination, on the other hand, can easily accept the birthplace.

IV

By the time they come to examine the symbols of the Nativity, the shepherds have completely lost their literalism and have developed a spiritual imagination. When they recognize the meaning in the burning bush, they know they have achieved a new order of vision:

> I PASTOR: That was for to se
> Hir holy vyrgynyté;
> That she vnfylyd shuld be—
> Thus can I ponder—
> And shuld haue a chyld sich was neuer sene.
> 2 PASTOR: Pese, man, thou art begyld: Thou shall se
> hym with eene. (364–69)

The parenthetical "thus can I ponder" indicates the shepherd's awareness of his new interpretive powers. The English present surrounding the shepherds suggests that this achievement is a spiritual condition, not an historical moment.

The shepherds' new depth in perception seems linked to the understanding of brotherhood that closes their feast. The brawl at the banquet ends when the shepherds realize that their discord results from the false premise that one man is better than another:

> 3 PASTOR: Ye be both knafys.
> I PASTOR: Nay, we knaues all: thus thynk me best, So,
> syr, shuld ye call. (277–79)

Cawley suggests that the shepherd is playing upon two meanings of "knave," the first pejorative and the second respectable.[31] In the context of the other Wakefield plays, particularly the *Mactacio Abel,* it is more likely an expression of brotherhood, especially since the exchange generates charity:[32] "For oure saules lett vs do / Poore men gyf it to" (283–84). The shepherds have learned what the gluttons in *Piers Plowman* never do, "Al is noȝt good to the gost • that the gut asketh."[33]

The dialogue about the extra bottle explains what had been missing in the banquet:

> 2 PASTOR: Yit a botell here is—
> 3 PASTOR: That is well spoken;
>   By my thryft, we must kys!!
> 2 PASTOR: —That had I forgoten. (261–63)

The fragmented sentence emphasizes the omission of the kiss rather than of the bottle. Lydgate explains the connection of the Kiss of Peace to the Nativity and the Lamb of God:

> Thys Agnus dei brought with hym pease
> To all the world at hys Natyuyte,
> Grace, gladnesse, of vertew gret encrease,
> For whyche the pepyll of hygh and low degre
> Kysse the pax, a tokyn of vnyte,
> Whyche kyssyng doth playnly signyfy
> How Pease ys cause of all felycyte
> Of folk gouernyd by prudent polycy.[34]

The shepherds soon cease their arguments—"furth let it rest; / we wil not brall" (279–80)—betokening with their kiss and charitable gestures the peace that is to come. They are now, echoing Vergil, fully prepared to envision a new image of the world:

> Saturne shall bend
> Vnto vs,
> With peasse and plenté,

> With ryches and menee,
> Good luf and charyté
> Blendyd amanges vs. (398–404)

The elaborate ceremony of making a cross marks the transition: They are no longer fools of the world, but fools for Christ. These were men who felt that "the warld is slyke; also helpars / is none here" (94–95). Now they entrust themselves to "Iesus onazorus, / Crucyefixus" (292–93). With their charity and their cross they have made, symbolically, the leap which makes fools of wise men and wise men of fools: "But we prechen Crist crucified, to Jewis sclaundre, and to hethene men foli; but to tho Jewis and Grekis that ben clepid, *we prechen* Crist the vertu of God and the wisdom of God" (1 Cor. 1:23–24).

With their new wisdom the shepherds come to offer gifts to the Child in the manger. These gifts, a spruce coffer, a ball, and a bottle, reflect on a literal level the shepherds' new sense of abundance, their understanding of a world which offers song and play as well as backbreaking work, and especially their homely joy in seeing the Child, but they also have a symbolic value which parallels the traditional meanings of the gifts of the Magi:[35]

> The kyngis browght þer offrynge,
> Gold þat betokneth a worthy kynge,
> Insens, pristhode; myr, buryinge
> For his manhode.[36]

Read in the context of this triad, the shepherds' gifts reflect the primary themes of the play. The ball parallels gold as a symbol of royalty. More specifically, it is the orb representing the world, and kingship,[37] both of which, the shepherds now know, are in the hands of Christ. The gift therefore signifies an end of their worries about the instability and oppression of the world. The coffer (coffin)[38] made of evergreen spruce[39] parallels the myrrh as a sign of Christ's sacrifice and promised resurrection. The *Stanzaic Life of Christ* elaborates the idea of "burying" in this way:

> Mirre also was ȝyuen oright,
> siþen he shuld degh & buriet be,
> to bavme hym, al-thaȝe he had tiȝt
> to rise from deth in daies thre.[40]

It is this sacrifice that will free those, including the shepherds, "that Adam had sold" (333).

The meaning of the third gift, the bottle, is slightly more elusive, but it too parallels the Magi's gifts and symbolically returns what Christ gives to man at His birth. In the play, the bottle is connected with the wisdom which inebriates man so that the third shepherd's "It is a good bowrde / For to drynke of a gowrde" (482–83) has spiritual overtones. According to tradition, not to be drunk with wisdom was to be a fool: "For wiþ-oute [the welle of witt and wisdom] þer nys philosphie ne oþer witt nouȝt worþ but pure folie, and þat witt put þe Holy Gost in-to þe herte whan he ȝeueþ þe ȝifte of wisdom . . . and ȝeueþ hym drynke and makeþ hym dronke of an holy love."[41] The bottle, then, represents the gift of wisdom, given to man at the manger, which freed him from misunderstanding the nature of "this world here":

> Than misericordia, that mercyfulle maye,
> Seyng mane was dampnde for hys trepas,
> hathe sent down sapiencia, þe soþe to saye
> Mane to redeme and bryng to grase.
>   Mirabilem misterium
>   þe sone of god ys mane be-cume.[42]

The bottle, symbolizing wisdom, parallels the gift of incense as a sign of priesthood, since the shepherds have now become preachers of Christ crucified.[43]

The shepherds' gifts affirm their new attitude toward the world. They realize that despite their unworthiness they have received an unparalleled gift. Their feeling of blessedness contrasts sharply with their earlier envy of them "that hens ar past!" (1):

> We had sene
> That many sant desyryd,
> With prophetys inspyryd;
> If thay hym requyryd,
> Yit closyd ar thare eene. (444–48)

The shepherds deeply appreciate the new vision that has been granted them.

Those chosen will often reverse expectation: "But God chees tho thingis that ben foltyesch of the world, that he confounde wyse men; and God chees the syke thingis, or freel, of the world, that he confounde the stronge thingis" (1 Cor. 1:27). It is not surprising that these shepherds, who had seemed fools in the ways of the world, can suddenly demonstrate such knowledge of prophetic lore. One may object that although these shepherds are not wise in the ways of the world, they are not unworldly like the Wakefield Abel. The playwright determined their character in relation to the theme of worldly uncertainty. The ideal fool would obviate the contrast between worldly and spiritual wisdom, since the unworldly man would not care about chance and disorder. The playwright chooses instead shepherds who begin with mundane concerns, so that their distress may be relieved when they understand the nature of temporality. A figure who began in the play as a fool for Christ would not mourn, "Wo is me this distres / And has no helpyng" (35–36) and could not then discover the joyful revelation of the Nativity:

> Nothyng is inpossybyll,
> Sothly, that God wyll;

It shal be stabyll
That God wyll haue done. (373–76)

The playwright has taken the traditional material of the adoration of the shepherds and welded it with folklore elements to produce a play in which the unstable, "penneles" world of chance is replaced by the eternal, plentiful Kingdom of Heaven. He transforms the Three Fools of Gotham into true wise men, who through their symbolic imagination are able to see spiritual meaning in earthly things and thus can free themselves, with the help of Christ, from the oppressiveness and uncertainty of the world.

V • Satan as Everyshepherd

COMIC METAMORPHOSIS IN *THE SECOND SHEPHERDS' PLAY*

The playwright's investigation of the symbolic imagination in the first shepherds' play suggests a reason for the existence of a second. When the play's literal fools become prophets of Christ, they have been symbolically transformed into players in an allegorical drama, so that even as *Prima pastorum* analyzes symbolic perception, it begins to slight the richness of the symbolic medium. In *Secunda pastorum,* talk of labor pains, strange apparitions, mystic circles, and changelings brings a sense of transformation that turns allegory into symbolism. Characters develop within themselves even as they become each other. Allegorical and folk elements clash and resonate to depict man's hopes and fears before the Nativity. A. P. Rossiter notes the tension but denies the fluidity: "We are left to wrestle with the uncombinable antinomies of the medieval mind: for these immiscible juxtapositions constantly imply two contradictory schemes of values, two diverse spirits; on standing for reverence, awe, nobility, pathos, sympathy; the other for mockery, blasphemy, baseness, meanness or spite, *Schadenfreude,* and derision. Above all, it is the fact that the 'other spirit' is *comic* that compels reflection and analysis; for the evaluated effect of the ambivalence reaches out towards searching irony."[1] In the play, the comic does compel reflection, but through the combination, not separation, of these antinomies.

The critics who allegorize Mak as a devil or antichrist tend to ignore the effect of the comic spirit upon allegory. Instead they freeze the characters in allegorical roles and deny the possibility of character development, or of the comic undermining of allegorical significance. On analogy with the lack of perspective in medieval art, these critics tend to think of the play as a drama of being rather than becoming. Even the most flexible member of this group, Francis Thompson, presents his evidence as if the Nativity and the pseudo-nativity were a pair of tableaux standing side by side.[2] The perspectiveless panel, however, which is usually used to demonstrate the stasis of medieval art, is often part of a series depicting the progress in the life of a saint or the development of a person in the holy family. In medieval literature similar growth occurs as allegorical figures encompass antagonistic meanings that merge into a single symbolic significance. The dreamer in *Piers Plowman,* a shepherd wrapped in a sheepskin, is both pastor and sheep, and the poem explores the interplay of these two roles on both the moral and the Christological level. The dreamer in *The Book of the Duchess,* a naïf sophisticate, becomes a physician for the Black Knight and for himself, as well. In the Wakefield play, as in these two examples, the sense of process and change operates constantly.

The critics who allegorize Mak isolate him in opposition to the shepherds and ignore the comic tone of his role. William Manley finds this bumbling villain to be the epitome of evil: "He is false while Christ is true, and this duality alone might well evoke the familiar Antichrist-Christ contrast in a medieval mind, if only subconsciously."[3] Eugene Zumwalt also sees the triumph of illusion in the machinations of Mak: "In the . . . play, the shepherds are fused as a unit posed against Mak, and the business of illusion is used as a complicating mechanism in the conflict of good and evil. In the introductory movements of the *Second Shepherds' Play*, the crude action of the rustics may be, to a spectator conscious of Christian morality, a microcosmic conflict of God-Christ and Lucifer."[4] From this viewpoint, the complaints of the shepherds exemplify the playwright's "critical, skeptical and humanistic spirit, which observes evils with a pervading, if not prevailing pessimism and questions fundamental religious conceptions,"[5] but neither critic allows the possiblity of character interaction or change.

John Speirs, on the other hand, emphasizes the play's folklore antecedents and reaches the opposite conclusion: "The mock-nativity does not appear to be introduced in the mocking spirit of scepticism. The boisterousness of the Mak farce as a whole, culminating in the tossing of Mak in a blanket, may rather be interpreted as an expression of the jollity of the folk as the rebirth significance of the midwinter festival overcomes the death significance."[6] Speirs reads the play's tone differently from the allegorists because he watches contrasting elements develop and merge, while they emphasize the antagonism of these elements. Four loci have to be critically examined to determine which position is correct: the gloomy, pessimistic complaints of the three shepherds; the confrontation between Mak and the shepherds; the allegorical role of Mak; and, finally, the tone of the Nativity play.

II

The gloomy opening of the play forms a background for the comic scenes, and its juxtaposition with them will help to establish the playwright's attitude toward his Nativity pageant. Eleanor Prosser dismisses this

prologue as mere realism and refuses to consider
whether or not it has any relation to the rest of the
play: "The value of the realistic details is historic, not
artistic. That is, Daw's complaint about the unjust
treatment of servants gives us a picture of fifteenth
century life; it may or may not serve a dramatic
function."[7] We cannot take this position. Rather we
must follow Speirs, who, in protest against the advocates of comic rather than realistic relief, voices an
objection which applies to Prosser's statement: "Less
than justice has been done to [the play] as significant
art, even by those who have praised it too simply as
farce, light comic relief intruded into the old solemn
nativity play. Instead it needs to be insisted that the
play is a poem."[8] Following Speirs, we must accept the
integrity of the play, and discover the relation of its
parts through imagistic and structural patterns.

The shepherds' anachronistic complaint about contemporary social ills has been called deeply pessimistic
because it reminds the audience that the world did not
change with the coming of Christ.[9] We must point out
that here, as in the *Prima pastorum,* the shepherds
suffer from hardships which represent spiritual as well
as physical barrenness. In every age Christ ameliorates
spiritual winter for all mankind. Physical change occurs, primarily as a hopeful symbol for the rest of
mankind, only in the generation of those who bear
witness to Christ. Another shepherds' play will illustrate this pattern.

In the Coventry play, the shepherds' complaints are
a simpler but more explicit symbolic prologue to the
Nativity. The physical condition of the first shepherd
represents the spiritual state of mankind before the
birth of Christ. The shepherd is lost, cold, and separated from his fellows:

Now God, that art in Trenete,
Thow sawe my fellois and me!
For I kno nott wheyre my scheepe nor the be,
Thys nyght ys soo colde.
Now ys yt nygh the myddis of the nyght;
These wedurs ar darke and dym of lyght,
Thatt of them can hy haue noo syght,
Standyng here on this wold.[10]

Manley's evocative description of the three shepherds in *Secunda pastorum* would fit here as well: "Each shepherd as he enters appears to be both physically sensitive to the cold and metaphysically sensitive to this pregnant moment in time."[11] Although the gloom of the weather and spirit in the Coventry play parallels that noted by Zumwalt in the Wakefield play, as in that play, it is the prologue to joy:

Brothur, myrth and solas ys cum hus among;
For be the swettnes of ther songe,
Goddis Sun ys cum, whom we haue lokid for long,
Asse syngnefyith thys star that we do see.[12]

In addition to the cold weather, the Wakefield shepherds' "metaphysical woe" arises from the barrenness of the land, the oppression of the "gentlery men," and the trials of fatherhood. All of these are interrelated as forces antagonistic to the springing forth of new life.

When the first shepherd begins to speak of farming and childbirth, images of sterility correspond to the low ebb of man's spiritual state. The winter overwhelms the shepherds and drains them of vitality. The barren land reflects their lack of vigor, and they have lost hope that anything will grow again: "No wonder, as it standys, if we be poore, / For the tylthe of oure landys lyys falow as the floore" (12–13). An early English lyric describing man's life also uses barren winter fields as an image of complete desperation:

> Wynter wakeneþ al my care,
> nou þis leues wakeþ bare;
> ofte y sike & mourne sare
> when hit comeþ in my þoht
> of þis worldes ioie hou hit geþ al to noht.
>
> ....
>
> al þat grein me graueþ grene
> nou hit faleweþ al by-dene—
> ihesu, help þat hit be sene
> ant shild vs from helle.[13]

The lyricist paints this bleak picture to counterpoint the joy in the hoped-for return of Christ, not to make his reader despair. The Wakefield Master also starts his play in the wintry reality of worldly suffering and death. The first two shepherds deepen their gloom by remembering that they are on the edge of the pit. The first shepherd is "nerehande dold" (2), while his companion laments that it is "now late in oure lyfys" (82). These are men whose desperate need for Christ is apparent in their weariness with life and life's processes.

The tone of debility spreads through the opening soliloquy as the shepherd fears that all activity will be abortive. Images of enervated submission, especially the reference to hamstringing, evoke man as a creature devoid of creative energy:

> We ar so hamyd,
> Fortaxed and ramyd,
> We ar mayde handtamyd
> With thyse gentlery men. (15–16)

The "gentlery men" stifle the shepherds because they restrict growth. Lack of fertility,[14] perhaps extended by a sexual metaphor, symbolizes the hopelessness of the winter landscape: "These men that ar lord-fest, thay cause the ploghe tary" (20).

The second shepherd, Gib, extends the theme of spiritual blight, as the complaint of "sely wedmen" (65) replaces that of "sely husbandys" (19). Fertility in marriage and in agriculture are linked by the word *husbandys,* which here means "farmer," but later (406) "spouse." Through imagery and metaphor, the second shepherd shows his disgust at marriage and childbearing. Gib's wife, who is "sharp as thystyll, as rugh as a brere" (101), becomes for him part of the barren landscape. As Cawley notes, his description of his hen in "labor" projects more fully his loathing of childbirth:[15]

> Sely Copyle, oure hen, both to and fro
> She kakyls;
> Bot begyn she to crok,
> To groyne or to clok,
> Wo is hym is oure cok,
> For he is in the shakyls. (67–72)

When man sees fatherhood as slavery, hope has almost disappeared from his vocabulary.

The powerful case against childbirth in a nativity play is not pessimistic.[16] Rather it works like the first part of a *débat,* in which the poet presents an almost convincing argument for the opposition before he produces his own evidence. Several songs in praise of the Virgin use misogyny as a prologue to Mariolatry.[17] In one, the poet tearfully repents the antifeminism which had been engendered by a woman not unlike Gyll, who, we realize by the end of the poem, is Eve:

> al wrong y wrohte for a wyf
> þat made vs wo in world ful wyde;
> heo rafte vs alle richesse ryf,
> þat durre vs nout in reynes ryde.[18]

The poet first presents the misogynistic position and then, as he reflects upon the place of Mary in human

salvation, he reverses his attitude radically. The lyricist responds particularly to the springing forth of life
and focuses on Mary's pregnancy:

> In hire lyght on ledeþ lyf,
> & shon þourh hire semly syde.
> þourh hyr side he shon
> ase sonne doþ þourh þe glas—
> wommon nes wicked non
> Seþþe he ybore was.[19]

The poet's tears purge his misogyny and leave him
joyous:

> Nou wo in world ys went a-way
> & weole is come ase we wolde
> þourh a mihti methful mai
> þat ous haþ cast from cares colde.[20]

As it does in the shepherds' play, the birth has re-
leased man from wintry cold.

In the Wakefield play, the transition from misogyny
to worship of the Virgin and child can occur when
Gyll's statements praising women—"Yit a woman
avyse helpys at the last" (342) and "Full wofull is the
household / That wantys a woman" (420–21)—become
valid. Although there is some pragmatic truth in the
proverbs because of Gyll's skillful handling of the deception, their true significance awaits the appearance
of Mary. The miraculous conception brings the allevia-
tion of woe, causing the once misogynistic shepherds
to join in a song of praise to women:

> Thay prophecyed by clergy—that in a vyrgyn
> Shuld he lyght and ly, to slokyn oure syn,
> And slake it,
> Oure kynde, from wo;
> For Isay sayd so:
> *Ecce Virgo*
> *Concipiet* a chylde that is nakyd. (676–82)

To reach this end of their dread of childbirth, the shepherds must rid themselves of the thoughts which equate wives with woe and life with pain.

III

The Mak episode is no excrescence, for the shepherds in this play, as in the *Prima pastorum,* must be spiritually ready to witness the greatest of miracles. Mak appears when they have finished their opening complaints, and he disappears after their mood has been changed sufficiently so that they are disappointed that Mak's heir has not been born.

Mak appears after, and almost in response to, the shepherds' song against cold and despair. Each song in the play (this one, Mak's lullaby, the angel's *gloria,* and the shepherds' two later songs)[21] marks a point of transformation, and this one is no exception. The shepherds have fallen into what *The Lay Folks Catechism* calls "wanhope."[22] To remove wanhope the shepherds must slough off their old ways; like the true Christian, they cast off the Old Man of non-Christian attitudes and put on the New. Their dealings with Mak center upon his embodiment of "old" life-denying attitudes which they themselves possess. Mak symbolizes the characteristics in the shepherds which prevent their seeing Christ. Mak has the second shepherd's misogyny and the third's slyness, and his claims to mastery over the first two parallel their ineffective attempt to bully their servant, Daw.

Mak's role is made clear by the costume in which he first comes on the scene. The direction "tunc intrat Mak in clamide se super togam vestitus" almost certainly means that Mak enters in the garb of the "gentlery men" about whom the first shepherd complains.

We must read the scene as the audience saw it: The first shepherd has complained about the gentlery men, he says things will get worse, they sing to keep things from getting worse, and a man (from his costume apparently one of the maintained men) appears. The "villain," however, turns out to be a clown who is unmasked after his first words. Mak personifies the thing the first shepherd fears most, yet it turns out to be far less fearsome than expected.

Mak, then, is the comic avatar of the shepherds' troubles, and his despair about childbirth is especially important in this nativity play. He complains bitterly about the number of mouths that he has to feed, and sighs loudly about the prospect of another:

> Lyys walteryng—by the roode—by the fyere, lo!
> And a howse full of brude. She drynkys well, to;
> Yll spede other good that she wyll do! (236–38)

Mak surpasses the negation of the second shepherd and adds a murderous wish to these cold thoughts:

> Now wyll ye se what I profer?—
> To gyf all in my cofer
> To-morne at next to offer
> Hyr hed-maspenny. (249–52)

Only by casting out the Mak in themselves can the shepherds expel the spiritual winter. The shepherds must transform Mak's desperate view of his condition, "Now wold God I were in heuen, for ther wepe no barnes / so styll" (193–94), into a positive yearning for Heaven, which also rejoices in earthly childbirth.

As an allegorical figure, Mak appears to be Satan, but on a less abstract plane, Mak is everyshepherd, in his greatest need for Christ. Talk of changelings and magic spells sets the mood for this identification, so that the shepherds' despair brings Mak to life: He appears only when the air is gravid with their complaints.

By questioning his identity—"Why who be ich?" (207)—Mak urges the audience to do the same. Then when Mak arises after having lain among the shepherds, he seems to become one of them: "Was I neuer a shephard, bot now wyll I lere" (288). The second shepherd unconsciously testifies to this transformation when he tells Mak, "Freyndes will we be, for we ar all oone" (566).

The need for the false nativity in purging the shepherds' "makness" can be seen by comparing this play with the Coventry analogue. Unlike their Wakefield counterparts, the Coventry shepherds are as ready as man can be to receive news of the Nativity. The first shepherd makes a magnificent gesture of brotherhood when he calls out, not to remedy his loneliness, but to relieve his companions' concern for him:

> But now to make there hartis lyght,
> Now wyll I full right
> Stand apon this looe,
> And to them cry with all my myght,—
> Full well my voise the kno.[24]

No charitable concern for others is exhibited by the Wakefield shepherds, who successively ignore each other as they enter. Gyb ignores Coll while addressing his misogynistic sermon to the audience, and is brusquely rebuked: "God looke ouer the raw! Full defly ye stand" (109). Daw, in turn, pokes fun at the two of them and turns on his heel in a curt gesture of isolation.[25]

The shepherds' second visit to Mak's cottage indicates a change of outlook. Before leaving the first time, the third shepherd exposes the similarity between the shepherds and Mak, when he remarks on Mak's lack of charity: "Fare wordys may ther be, bot luf is ther none / þis yere" (569–70). When the shepherds leave they immediately discover that they have failed to leave a gift. With this recognition of their own lapse in charity they return, hoping to see the new child.

In spite of their suspicions, Mak's son becomes an object of delight for the shepherds. They have a chance to call back their original misogynistic notions and a bright spark of hope peeps through in a greeting that will be made again to the Christ child: "The child will it not grefe, that lytyll day-starne" (577). The shepherds' complaint about "hee frawde" (594) is as much a reflection of their disappointment that a child has not been born as a remark about the sheep that has been stolen.

The tossing of Mak has been specifically related to the birth imagery by Claude Chidamian, who remarks, "They toss Mak for his sin of sheep-stealing and the greater sin of deception in the false child-birth."[26] Chidamian cites the text of the medieval midwife, Trotula, to demonstrate that "it is just by this method of tossing that primitive and medieval peoples hastened delivery in childbirth."[27] The midwife's instructions provide a second interpretation which will be more consistent with the idea of catharsis in the play: "Colphon says to let the limbs be shaken to break the bag of water and in this way the foetus will come forth. *Thus also those may be aided who are laboring to bring forth a dead foetus:* Let the patient be placed in a linen cloth stretched by four men at the four corners with the patient's head somewhat elevated. Let the four corners be strongly drawn this way and that by the opposite corners and she will give birth immediately, God favoring her."[28] The alternative of the use of tossing as a way to induce a stillbirth may be more instructive here, in view of the third shepherd's specific instructions:

> For this trespas
> We will nawther ban ne flyte,
> Fyght nor chyte,
> Bot haue done as tyte,
> And cast hym in canvas. (624–28)

The word "cast" has special significance in reference to abortion as is noted in a medieval obstetric manual: "or when the materie is makyng aborte i. castyng childe."[29]

With the tossing of Mak, all things that he symbolizes become stillborn and the shepherds can proceed to the Nativity. Mak disappears from the action immediately upon his being tossed in the blanket, and the shepherds groan as if they, not he, had undergone the punishment. Their plainsong had ushered Mak in, and now the angel's *Gloria* marks his exit.[30]

IV

The Wakefield Master's handling of the Satanic analogy supplements the comic effect created by the shepherds' rejection of Mak. While Mak tries and pretends to be dangerous, he never succeeds. One must look carefully at Mak's allegorical role as Devil or, as Manley sees it, Antichrist. Mak is satanic in his claims of mastery, in his role as magician, in the wolf imagery which surrounds him, and as a deceiver, but in each case he undercuts the terror of Satan through his own ineptitude.

The opening complaint about "gentlery men" fits a play which allegorizes Mak as the "enemy" of man, but the difference between Mak and the "gentlery men" cannot be ignored. If there are any effective devils in the physical world of the play, they are these "lord-fest" (20) men. They have the pride of Lucifer,

"ther shall com a swane as prowde as a po" (37), and
much of his danger as well. Mak tries to ape the
"maystry" of these oppressors who in turn are supported "thrugh mantenance / of men that ar gretter"
(35–36), but his ruse is quickly detected. His failure
to impress with his outlandish "Sothren tong"[31] re-
duces him and the Devil he represents from evil power
to comic bungler. The audience had already seen Satan forfeit his place in the divine hierarchy by striving
for the same mastery coveted by Mak:

> Certys, it is a semely sight
> Syn that we ar all angels bright,
> and euer in blis to be;
> if that ye will behold me right,
> this mastre longys to me.[32]

Satan's fall and the beginning of evil stem from his
failure to grasp the paradoxical concept of equality in
hierarchy.

Mak and the shepherds also have not yet learned
that acceptance of temporal and eternal degree does
not imply that one man is in any real sense set above
another. The playwright uses the parable of the work-
ers in the vineyard to counterbalance Mak's illegiti-
mate claims to mastery. Mak misapplies the parable
when he gives the stolen sheep to his wife:

> For in a strate can I gett
> More then thay that swynke and swette
> All the long day. (311–13)

The parable does not mean that man can abdicate
responsibility for his actions, but it does promise eternal equality for those presently oppressed: "Therefore
in that reward we shall all be equal . . . because that
denarius is eternal life and in eternal life all shall be
equal."[33] Gyb denies the parable when he refuses to
let Daw eat:

> What, the boy lyst raue! Abyde vnto syne;
> We haue mayde it.
> Yll thryft on thy pate!
> Though the shrew cam late,
> Yit is he in state
> To dyne—if he had it. (148–53)

The conclusion of the parable, "so shall the last be first and the first last," should be the hope of these shepherds on the bottom of the wordly chain of degree. Daw in particular has much to hope for, since he is at the very bottom of the pecking order: "Sich seruandys as I, that swettys and swynkys, . . . / We are oft weytt and wery when master-men wynkys" (154, 156). The reversal of order at the end of the play symbolizes the realization of the parable. The tossing of Mak is done at Daw's "reede" (624) and his words before they sleep assume a new tone of command. The third shepherd has become first—"Do my reede . . . do as I say you" (624, 637)—and Mak's presumption has been punished.

Mak's pretense of having satanic power is extended into his playing at magician. The casting of the circle around the shepherds is part of his role as "nigromancer,"[34] but the effect is hardly black magic; the weary shepherds are already asleep. Moreover, Mak bungles this role: the mystic circle is associated not with black magic but with white, as a way to protect man against the Devil.[35] Mak enjoys playing the Devil, just as he would have enjoyed being a "gentlery man." Francis Thompson says that Mak "is ludicrous as well as fearsome, and the second and third shepherds, though both recognize something unholy about this impenitent thief, give us reason to believe that we should be amused, not impressed with his threats."[36] Mak is not a sinister figure disguised as a clown, but rather a hopeless clown trying to borrow some dignity anywhere, even from Satan.

Gyll's greeting to Mak confirms this view; the imagery makes Mak the Deceiver, but her tone removes his fearsomeness: "Then may we se here the dewill in a bande, / Syr Gyle" (407–8). Mak may be Sir Guile, but he is still more the uxorious husband. Furthermore, it is not his guile but the schemes of his domineering wife that deceive the shepherds for a short while. If Mak is a devil, he is like the henpecked one in the folk tale who could not stand a blabbering woman.[37] Throughout the sheep-hiding episode it is he, not the shepherds, who sweats with fear.

The final image pattern for Mak as Devil is that of wolf. The wolf is commonly allegorized in the bestiaries as the Devil: "The wolf is rarely found to have a good meaning but very often the opposite. For he signifies the Devil as in this example from scripture: 'He saw the wolf coming, and left his sheep, and fled.' "[38] Mak seizes the sheep in a particularly wolfish manner:

> Now were tyme for a man that lakkys what he wold
> To stalk preuely than vnto a fold.
> And neemly to wyrk than, and be not to bold. (270–72)

The *Physiologus* tells us that the wolf snares its prey in a similar sneaky way: "The wolf approaches the sheepfold like a tame dog, and lest the watchdogs smell its evil breath and awaken the shepherds, it goes against the wind."[39] The third shepherd, who, as usual, is aware of what is going on, almost identifies Mak as a wolf: "Me thoght he was lapt in a wolfe-skyn" (368). Mak does not, however, quite carry off the wolf image. The wolf of the bestiaries is "a rapacious beast, greedy for slaughter."[40] Furthermore, "they go hungry for a long time."[41] Mak has the hunger of the bestiary wolves—"This twelmothe was I not so fayn of oone shepe-mete" (324)—but unlike the wolves ("and after

long fasting, they devour a great deal")[42] he is unable
to satisfy his raging belly.

With the image "lapt in a wolfe-skyn," the Wakefield Master identifies Mak according to his own
lights. The next line, "So ar many hapt now, namely
within" (369), warns us to look carefully; this is a
twisted allusion to Matthew (7:15). Mak, because of
his troubles, takes on the form, but never the viciousness, of a predator. He becomes the nonproverbial
sheep in wolf's clothing. It is fitting that such a man
should claim a sheep for his son.

This inversion of Mak's role allows us to view the
pseudo-Nativity as an integral part of a play which
celebrates the true Nativity. Chambers, somewhat
amazed at the audacity of the playwright, registers
shock at the sheep-finding episode: "There follows
what can only be described as an astonishing parody of
the Nativity itself."[43] What then are we to make of
Homer Watt's claim that the parody enhances the Nativity? "In the Mak episode . . . the sheep-hiding details . . . produce a perfect burlesque of the charming
Christ child scene that concludes the play."[44]

The difficulty can be resolved if one remembers that
both Chambers and Watt are reading the play as critics would and not viewing the play as the audience
does. One must realize that it is almost impossible to
see the Mak episode as parody or burlesque of the
Nativity until one gets to the end of the play. Only
someone with the playwright's imagination would immediately see the sheep in Mak's cottage as the new-
born Lamb. The audience would see the scene as the
shepherds do—as a disappointing burlesque of human
childbirth, but not yet as one of the Nativity.

This is not to say that it would be difficult for the
director to make the relationship of the scenes clear.
The primary device would be the parallel staging of

the two scenes. If the group of cradle, mother, and
shepherds offering a gift are arranged in the same po-
sitions for each episode, the parallel would be instantly recognized *when* the Nativity scene repeats the
tableau of the shepherds' reentering Mak's cottage. It
is even possible that the same place is used for both
scenes, so that Mak's cottage is transformed into the
manger. The sheep's cradle, now flanked by representations of the two beasts, would then become the crib
of the Christ child. Whether one place or two are
used, both cottage and manger must appear equally
wretched so that the audience will realize that the difference is in the spirit of love that pervades the second. This might well be pointed up by the unnamed
song that the shepherds sing as the play ends. Since
Mak has opened the scene in his cottage with a tune-
less lullaby and Mary has instructed the shepherds to
"tell furth as ye go" (744) the miracle they have witnessed, it is likely that their song would be a lullaby
carol describing the event. A fairly common contemporary carol, which first wonders at the wretchedness
of the manger and then explains it, would be the kind
of song they might sing:

> This endurs nyght
> I see a syght,
> A sterne schone bryght as day,
> And euer ymong
> A meden song
> Was, "By, by, lulley."
>
> This louely lady sete and song,
> And tyll hur chyld con say,
> "My Son, my Lord, my Fadur dere,
> Why lyus thou thus in hey?
> Myn one swete bryd,
> What art thou kyd
> And knowus the Lord of ey?
> Neuerthelesse

> I will not sesse
> To syng, 'By, by, lulley.' "
>
> This chyld ontyll is modur spake,
> And thus me thowght he seyd:
> "I am kend for Heuun Kyng
> In cryb thowgh I be leyd.
> Angeles bryght
> Shall to me lyght,
> Ye wot ryght welle, in fey."[45]

Such a song might well balance Mak's "lullay" that is "crooned" to the accompaniment of Gyll's groaning.

Parody (or burlesque) misrepresents the dramatic relationship of the two scenes. To understand the effect of the play, one must see the Nativity scene as an "unparody" of the sheep-hiding scene. This is to agree with Watt that the Nativity is a beautification of the ugly, but the scene in Mak's cottage cannot be a debasement of the beautiful, because it can be recognized as a parallel only after the appearance of the scene parodied.

The Mak episode, therefore, reminds us of the theme of the play, which is announced in the first words of the Angel:

> Ryse, hyrd-men heynd, for now is he borne
> That shal take from the feynd that Adam had lorne;
> That warloo to sheynd, this night is he borne. (638–40)

The coming in glory is to be contrasted with the abortive travail for "Makys ayre" (604). Yet even here the playwright maintains his sympathetic ambiguity; the "hornyd lad" (601) is as much sheep as devil. Since the visit to Mak's cottage prepares the shepherds for the Nativity by enlarging their sympathy, "Makys ayre" does, in a sense, become "a yong lad / For to mend oure flok" (387–88). As father of the sheep, Mak is absorbed by the shepherds. Only in his negative roles, as desperate human being or deceptive thief, must the Mak in man be cast out.

The Nativity scene testifies to the accomplishment of this goal. As has been noted, the set may be Mak's cottage slightly refurbished or another set very much like it in its physical wretchedness: "He was poorly arayd / Both mener and mylde" (690–91). The shepherds see through the misery of the scene and their own previous pessimism as they present their gifts. Several critics have pointed out that the gifts symbolize aspects of Christ and are meant to parallel the symbolic value of the gifts of the Magi.[46] The gifts are also symbolic statements of the shepherds' freedom from the woeful complaints that opened the play.

Each gift is emblematic of the way the birth of the Christ child has transformed the attitude of the shepherds, and has a specific appropriateness to the shepherd who gives it. The first shepherd, who had complained about the barrenness of the land, gives an emblem of unwonted fertility in midwinter—the bob of cherries.[47] The second shepherd, who had used a shackled rooster as an image of marriage and fatherhood, presents a bird as a symbol of freedom. The third shepherd, who saw his life as an unending misery of sweaty toil, offers the ball as a sign that man can play as well as work in the world. The gifts, then, have the same relation to the complaints as the Nativity does to the Mak episode.

VI • Herod As Antichrist

PARODY BECOMES ALLEGORY

The Wakefield Master's most traditional use of allegory occurs in the *Magnus Herodes*. As a reviser of the cycle, the playwright was well aware of the typological significance attached to a number of the other tyrants in the plays. Walter Meyers has shown that many of the villains in this cycle carry specifically satanic attributes.[1] The Herod play surpasses the others because of the refinement of the satanic allegory to that of Antichrist, which it then works out with precise detail.

The dramatic tension in *Magnus Herodes* develops out of a conflict between Herod and Christ, who never appears on stage yet is always present. In *Coliphizacio* the Wakefield Master creates similar tension by using the silence of Christ to answer the bluster of his enemies. In the Herod play he accomplishes this task by converting Herod, through dramatic situation and allusion, into a figure of Antichrist. As Antichrist, Herod parodies the actions of Christ and becomes a constant reminder of his presence. In developing the equation, Herod = Antichrist = imitation Christ (not *imitatio Christi*), the play examines the implications of parody as both imitation and perversion of an action.

The Wakefield Master builds his characterization of Herod as Antichrist upon the commonly held assumption that the murderer of the Innocents was a type of Satan: "Herod, who instigated the slaughter of the Innocents, represents the Devil or those people who, desiring to abolish the name of Christ from the world, wrathfully bring about the death of martyrs."[2] Herod was more specifically equated with the beast of Revelation through his likeness to Behemoth, a ruler over proud men: "There is another interpretation of Herod. I speak of Behemoth whom the Lord in his scripture calls mightily armed, 'whose strength is in his loins and whose power is in the navel of his belly,' 'surveying all high things, he is king over all the sons of pride.' He reigns now over the earth, and powerfully exercises his tyranny, this prince of the world, this ancient serpent, who is called the Devil and Satan."[3] The tradition noted, furthermore, that the city of Antichrist, like Herod's Jerusalem, was to be the capital of "maumentri":

> Right sua sal þe feind him þis
> Chese him stede o birth iwise, . . .
> A tun o selcuth mikel pride,
> Hefd o maumentri þat tide;
> Bethsaida and corozaim,
> þir tua cites sal foster him.[4]

The Wakefield Master seems aware of this tradition, since this is the only one of his plays in which the forces of evil invoke Mahowne (four times, at lines 1, 10, 54, 127) rather than Satan.[5] Finally, the crisis of the play, the slaughter of the Innocents, has been seen as the first act of the Antichrist: "The first act of the serpent was when, according to Matthew, murderous Herod sought the life of the newly born child, as was noted before, and on account of him killed the infants."[6] These citations suggest a viable tradition into which the playwright could build his characterization of Herod as Antichrist. The elaboration of this character relies heavily, as we shall see, upon the specific details from the literature of Antichrist.

II

The two primary tasks of the Antichrist are to invert all the laws of Christ and to imitate his power and place as the Messiah. Of the first, Adso, in his epistle *Concerning the Antichrist,* remarks:

> Therefore, you should first know of the Antichrist why he is given this name. Certainly it is because he shall be contrary to Christ in all things, that is, he shall do the opposite of what Christ does. Christ comes humbly, and he will come in pride. Christ comes to raise the humble and to do justice to sinners; he, on the other hand, will cast down the humble, glorify the sinner, exalt the ungodly and always teach those vices which are contrary to virtues.[7]

This describes Herod, but since it also describes any unrepentant sinner, the second characteristic, specific imitation of Christ, is needed to make Herod Antichrist. Herod, like Antichrist, combines the two features of inversion and imitation so that, even as he is acting in every possible manner against Christ and his laws, he is busy appropriating the titles of Christ and parodying his works.

In imitation of Christ, the Antichrist sends preachers of his word throughout the world. He claims Christ's title, his name, his gift of grace, his reign for all time and in all places, and finally his power over life and death. As the subverter of Christ, the Antichrist denies Jesus and his gospel, uses violence rather than love to establish his kingdom, promotes idolatry, and ultimately denies the resurrection. We shall see that the Wakefield Master gives all of these specific attributes to Herod.

The entrance of Nuntius begins Herod's imitation of Antichrist and parody of Christ. The Antichrist also sends out his messengers to preach his coming:

siþen ouer all þis werlde wide.
he salle sende sande with mikil pride
His preychours for to spel his wil.[8]

The Wakefield Master would find a pattern for his
parody of this feature in the story of John the Baptist,
which immediately follows the biblical text of the
Slaughter of the Innocents. Nuntius speaks to the
crowd:

> Take tenderly intent
> What sondys ar sent,
> Els harmes shall ye hent,
> And lothes you to lap.
>
> ....
>
> Luf hym with lewté;
> Dred hym, that doughty;
> He chargys you be redy
> Lowly at his lykyng. (6–10, 15–19)

These admonitions could easily pass for a medieval
version of the Baptist's message of obedience in the
face of the coming Judgment, a warning which the
audience would soon hear repeated in the play of John
the Baptist.[9] Not only does Nuntius parody the voice
in the desert, crying out for man to prepare for the
coming of the kingdom, he also parallels the Antichrist's threat that he will destroy all those who believe in Christ;

> To ierusalem salle he siþen fare.
> alle þat he cristen findis þare.
> if þai turne noȝt til his lare.
> he salle ham sle wiþ-outen spare.[10]

As Antichrist, Herod must take Christ's name.[11]
Nuntius renames Herod by identifying him with epi-
thets belonging to Christ. The first description of
Herod as the "heynd kyng . . . of Iury, sourmontyng

sternly with crowne" (10–11), suggests Christ on the Cross with his crown of thorns.[12] Nuntius also speaks of Herod in words of endearment strange for a king, but perfectly fitting for the Christ child: "He is the worthyest of all barnes that ar borne" (55) and the words preceding the entrance of Herod constitute a traditional *ave:* "Hayll, the worthyest of all!" (71).[13] The usurpation of title grows more direct when Nuntius praises the magnificence of Herod: "He is kyng of kyngys . . . / chefe lord of lordyngys" (37–38). These epithets describe Christ in Revelation 19:16, ironically at the moment when Christ is about to destroy the Antichrist.[14]

In order to give Herod the stature of Antichrist, Nuntius raises his rank. No longer merely king in Jerusalem, Herod becomes a maker of kings who controls "both kyng with crowne and barons of brith" (3). In the *Cursor mundi* Antichrist requires obedience from nobles of similar rank:

> þe grete kaisers & þe kingis.
> & suche oþer mani lordingis.
> turne þai salle til him before.[15]

The strange list of Herod's dominions is another part of the Antichrist legend and is closely related to his domination over kings. Herod is claiming sovereignty over all places and all times (from Eden to contemporary England), "From Paradyse to Padwa, to Mownt Flascon, / From Egyp to Mantua, vnto Kemptowne" (46–47), which parallels Antichrist's boast of rule over the whole earth: "Fra see to bank fra norþ to souþ / he salle do make his sarmoun couþ."[16] Meyers notes that Herod's claim to rule seventeen kingdoms corresponds to the seventeen kings who come under Antichrist's sway in Revelation.[17]

Herod's presumption that he will reign in all ages is

even more germane to the theme of the play. Arnoul Greban's treatment of the story most explicitly characterizes Herod as the king who refuses to recognize that his reign is only temporary. The French Herod responds to reports of the Nativity with boasts that no rival will ever displace him, nor will he be caught up in the fall of princes:

> Fortune, there's nothing to you.
> Fortune, you astonishing beast,
> I'll make you and your hateful wheel
> Turn the worse, by damn![18]

The Wakefield Herod also believes that he can escape from death and the turn of Fortune's wheel. This claim, together with his hopes to establish his name forever, parodies Christ's reign *in saecula saeculorum*. Herod's rage begins when he sees limits encroaching upon him:

> My name spryngys far and nere: the doughtyest men me
>   call,
> That euer ran with spere, a lord and kyng ryall.
> What ioy is me to here a lad to sesse my stall! (109–111)

Antichrist is the model of those who would establish lasting dominion in the world: "Antichrist, indeed, attempts to establish his fame on earth, since he seeks, were it possible, to live forever through worldly glory. He rejoices in celebrating his name in the marketplace, when he spreads far and wide his evil work. But because this evil of his has not been granted a long reign, it is said his fame shall perish from the earth, and his name will not be celebrated in the marketplace."[19] Herod, then, follows Antichrist in claiming Christ's name, power, and place for himself.

The inverse of these claims is the denial of Christ. When Herod's Nuntius says of Jesus, "a kyng thay hym call, and that we deny" (28), he is following in the footsteps of Antichrist: "This is the Antichrist, who denies the Father and the Son" (I John 2:22). Herod further denies Christ in his conference with his scholars. The medieval schools divided learning into sacred and profane letters. Scholars might use the classics, but never in their own right, only to explicate sacred writings. In a conservative expression of this view, Jerome condemns all classical writers: "What fellowship can there be between light and darkness? What agreement between Christ and Belial? What has Horace to do with the Psalter, or Vergil with the Gospels, or Cicero with the Apostle?"[20] Herod advocates this division, but from the opposite side. He forbids his investigators to read saints' lives or religious writings. Instead, he orders them to use only profane authors as the source of truth.

> Syrs, I pray you inquere in all wrytyng,
> In Vyrgyll, in Homere, and all other thyng
> Bot legende.
> Sekys poecé-tayllys,
> Lef pystyls and grales;
> Mes, matyns noght avalys—
> All these I defende. (201–7)

In prohibiting the use of the Bible and the Mass, Herod fulfils another role of the Antichrist, who,

> alle gode thew wiþ miȝt & maine
> he salle were ham a-gaine.
> þe gosspel & alle haly writte
> he salle for-do wa worth his witte.[21]

The Wakefield Master borrows the wise men from the previous Herod play (*Oblacio Magorum*) in the cycle, where they also cite the prophecies of Isaiah and Micah.[22] In that play, however, Herod rants and curses, but does not attempt to deny their tidings. The Wakefield Master adds Herod's debate with the wise men so that the scene also parodies Jesus' confrontation with the doctors in the play of that name, which is the second play after this one. Like the doctors, Herod's learned men cite the etymology of "Emanuel" as evidence of the coming of Christ. Like Christ in *The Doctors,* Herod argues that his councilors must look past the letter of the law.

III

The play's emotional impact comes from the Wakefield Master's ability to match Herod's psychology with the external signs of his role. The inner dimension corresponds to the medieval thinking that saw Antichrist both as the beast in Revelation and

> quatkin man sim-euer hit is
> out of þe rewle of riʒtwisnes.
> auther lewed or religioun.
> clerk or monk, or ellis canoun.
> & destrois at þai sulde were.
> of antecrist þe name salle bere.[23]

Gregory the Great explains that men living before Antichrist might share in his role by acting like him. Such men, Gregory says, are the physical members through which Antichrist performs his evils until his actual coming.[24] The extension of the Antichrist to an antichrist makes the members of the audience candidates for the latter role. Those who share Herod's self-deceit are destined to share his fate.

In imitation of Christ's establishment of the seat of Peter, Herod promises to make the second *consultus* a pope. By making this a position of secular power, Herod reveals his inversion of worldly and spiritual values. The word *grace*—"by grace of Mahowne," "gracyus you gretyng" (10, 13)—with its implications of divine love, is continually used of and by this parody of Christ. The misappropriation of the gift of grace is a specific act of the Antichrist, as in the Tegernsee play, where the Antichrist admonishes his followers: "Live in grace and receive honor, while you acknowledge the creator of all things."[25] Throughout the Wakefield cycle, grace is the only gift that man requires. In this play, for example, we are told that the Nativity will bring grace into the world: "Of Bedlem a gracyus lord shall spray, / That of Iury myghtyus kyng shal be ay" (219–20), and in the *Prima pastorum* the second shepherd begs of Christ, "bot oone drop of grace at my nede!"[26] Herod's brand of grace is meant to rival Christ's: "For this nobyll tythand thou shall haue a drope / Of my good grace" (265–66), but his grace is the world, carefully measured out:

> Markys, rentys, and powndys,
> Greatt castels and groundys;
> Thrugh all sees and soundys. (267–69)

This wordly grace is exactly what Antichrist promises his followers:

> And, for youre Regnis be but small,
> Cities, castells shall you befall,
> With Townes and Towres gay.[27]

After the slaughter has been carried out, Herod graphically spells out his grace:

> A hundreth thowsand pownde is good wage for a knyght;
> Of pennys good and rownde, now may ye go light
> With store. (444–46)

The payment of pounds in pence[28] shows that Herod is weighing them down with the things of this world, and the irony of "may ye go light" is intensified thirty lines later, when he speaks of the lightness of his soul. In a poem on the virtues of the Mass, Lydgate reminds us that lightness of soul can only be bought through the shedding of Christ's blood: "O thow my soule, how mayst thow heuy be, / Syth Cryst hath boght the with hys passion?"[29]

Herod's confident belief that "grace" is his to distribute leads to an even clearer example of his self-deceit. As soon as he appears on stage, Herod promises to fulfill his role as Antichrist by doing the opposite of everything that Christ will do: "For if I begyn, I breke ilka bone, / And pull fro the skyn the carcas anone" (84–85). Herod conceives of himself as Death stripping flesh from the bones. The role of Christ, according to the Chester Antichrist play, is to restore man from the condition in which Herod intends to leave him. Christ will begin with the bones: "He would revive them sone in hye, / With flesh and Sinew and Skynn therby."[30] The doctrine of the resurrection of the body severely limits Herod's death-dealing power, as the Wakefield audience will see in the raising of Lazarus and the harrowing of Hell.

Herod's claim, "in me standys lyfe and dede" (92) echoes the Antichrist's illusory ability to raise the dead. The Antichrist's claim, like Herod's, has no substance:

> To raise þe dede for mannis siȝt
> squa selcouþli to shew his miȝt . . .
> bot alle suche signis wrogt with art
> of soþfastnes salle haue na part.[31]

Herod quickly reveals that his control is only over death, "who that is so bold, I brane hym thrugh the hede!" (93), but forgets he controls only the death of others. He makes the same mistake as the rulers in *de casibus* tragedies, "I thynk not for to flytt, bot kyng I will be seyn / For euer" (175–76). After the slaughter, however, Herod lets slip the fact of his mortality:

> Had I bot oone bat at that lurdan
> So yong,
> It shuld haue bene spokyn
> How I had me wrokyn,
> Were I dede and rotyn
> With many a tong. (490–95)

Only Christ, the Chester play notes, can restore rotting flesh, but this will occur only after the destruction of Antichrist and the coming of Judgment:

> Beleus this fully, withouten wene,
> that all, which dead and rotten bene,
> in flesh shall ryse, as shalbe sene.[32]

IV

If the Wakefield play intends to show the nature and results of Herod's viciousness, why is this the only play of the English cycles extant in which Herod appears to remain in control at the end? The York play ends with Herod's enraged discovery that Christ has escaped his soldiers and in both the *Ludus Coventriae* and Chester versions, Death carries Herod off. The Chester playwright makes the Slaughter of the Innocents itself Herod's punishment by including Herod's son among the victims:

> SECUNDA MULIER: loe! lord loke and see!
>   the child that thou toke to me,
>   men of thy owne meny
>   haue slayn it, here the bene.
> HERODES (irabit): but it is vengeanc, as drink I wyne,
>   and that is now well sene.[33]

The French playwright Arnoul Greban also includes the death of Herod's son in his *Mystère de la Passion*, and adds a vivid description of Herod's torment as living death.[34]

These playwrights refuse to allow their audience to contemplate, even briefly, the triumph of evil. Instead they use the instant manifestation of justice to show that evil does not pay. The Chester and French versions explain most literally the idea that Herod reaped his own destruction through the Slaughter of the Innocents: "Herod falls screaming into the trap which he himself set, and unsheathes the evil which he plans."[35] In contrast, the Wakefield Herod's rage has passed at the end of the play and he comments brightly: "so light is my saull / that all of sugar is my gall!" (474–75). The Wakefield Master avoids overt didacticism and relies on the implications of the Antichrist legend and his characterization of Herod to provide his moral.

The Antichrist's apparent success, a feature that the Wakefield Master borrows for Herod, is basic to the lesson implied in his permitted existence. For Antichrist as for the Wakefield Herod, judgment comes unseen, not by the intervention of manifest force: "Daniel and Paul say the same thing about the Antichrist: He will rise up against the King of Kings and be destroyed without a hand being laid upon him. He will be destroyed, to be sure, not by a hand, because he will be struck down to eternal death, not by a war of angels, not by an onslaught of saints, but, when he comes, by a breath only from the mouth of the Judge."[36] One must understand the necessary defeat of the Antichrist and his members without expecting to witness it.

Although the Wakefield Master suspends Herod's external punishment, he signifies Herod's present torment in his hollow fury and his future torment in his role as Antichrist. Herod's image for his anger names the punishment that he fears most:

> Sich panys hard neuer man tell,
> For-vgly and for-fell,
> That Lucyfere in hell
> Thare bonys shall all to-tyre. (139–44)

The French play stages these torments,

> Alas! What unendurable torments:
> I see more than a hundred thousand devils,
> More hideous than one can imagine,
> Who wait for me, only so they can take me
> And drag me off with them,[37]

but the Wakefield Master does not want such facile retribution; his audience must recognize Herod's fear and expect, but not witness, his ultimate punishment.

Herod's terror of losing his "mastry" over life and death shows itself in the wrath that also characterizes him as Antichrist. Enoch, in the Chester *De adventu Antichristi,* notes this trait:

> Til we hard tokeninge
> of this Thefes cominnge,
> that now on Earth is rayginnge
> and doth gods folke destroy.[38]

The rage of Antichrist contains hidden consolation for man, since its growth marks its imminent cessation: "The Devil will rage more bitterly, the closer he comes to the torment of his reckoning."[39] The Wakefield Master has produced a psychological counterpart to this consolation, since the audience becomes aware that the more Herod rages the more he is losing his grasp on the situation. The language with which Herod berates the soldiers who have not found the Magi—"Fy, losels and lyars! lurdans ilkon! / Tratoures and well wars! knafys, bot knyghtys none" (163–64)—parallels almost exactly that used by the Antichrist to deny the charges

of Enoch and Elias in the Chester play: "O! You hipo-
crytes that so cryen! / lozells! Lordans! lowdly you
lyen!"[40]

Herod, like Cain, vents his fear in murder. Although his rage erupts in the violent slaughter of the
children, the murder, like everything else in the play,
has the veneer of control. The staging of the slaughter
is far more formal than in the other Herod plays. In
those plays, the scene is one of brawling chaos, but in
this play, the murders are almost ritualized. Each of
the three soldiers argues with a different woman, who
in turn beats him, then he kills her child, and she
responds with lamentation and finally a cry for vengeance. Each of these exchanges is almost the same
length (twenty-one to twenty-three lines) and has exactly the same pattern. The lament and call for re-
venge are part of the traditional grief of Rachel, and
the stylization of the scene makes the women's plaints
hauntingly effective.

Vengeance is forthcoming because it is implicit in
the judgment upon the Antichrist, as Herod reminds
the audience by calculating the number of his victims:

> A hundreth thowsand, I watt, and fourty ar slayn,
> And four thowsand. Therat me aght to be fayn;
> Sich a morder on a flat shall neuer be agayn. (487–89)

This is the number of those signed with the seal of
Christ in Revelation 7:4. This means that the Innocents will not only be saved, but also that it is necessary that this number of martyrs be completed before
the prayers of those in heaven can be answered. Thus
Herod's slaughter is not only to be avenged by Christ,
but becomes part of the divine plan. As Enoch remarks in the Chester play, the Antichrist is he who has
been suffered to destroy God's children. The play suggests that mankind cannot hurry God's justice.

In the Laon *Officium stellae,* an early liturgical version of the Herod play, the cry of the innocent children, "Why don't you prevent the shedding of our blood?" is answered by an angelic assurance: "Bear up a short time until the number of your brothers is fulfilled!"[41] The inconsolable Rachel is comforted by the *consolatrix,* who reminds her that life on earth is of limited importance: "Why dost thou mourn? Why dost thou sorrow? Exult! / For thy offspring shall dwell in blessedness above the stars."[42] The Wakefield Master does not project such an unworldly tone. As in other plays he knows how hunger gnaws despite spiritual sustenance, so here he captures the immediate grief that seizes the mothers of the murdered children. The consolation in this play does not take effect at once and can be fully absorbed only when one removes himself from the particular circumstance so that he can comprehend the overall scheme.

The Wakefield Master, through Herod's absurd claims that he will rule forever, has adumbrated the idea of the short time until consolation. Herod's wrath signifies that he has lost control of the situation. This wrath increases as he unconsciously recognizes that the end of his power is near at hand. Such is the behavior of the Antichrist as well: "Indeed, he carefully considers that what may come next will cause him to give up the freedom of his most malicious license, and the more he is constricted by the brevity of time, the greater he shall grow in the multiplication of cruelty, as John was told by that angelic voice: 'Woe to the land and the sea, for the Devil will descend upon you full of wrath, knowing he has but a brief stay.' "[43] Even as the destruction spreads, therefore, the believer can take comfort in the knowledge that the reign of Antichrist is near its end.

V

The Wakefield Master builds a similar consolation into Herod's triumph. An examination of the scene that follows the Slaughter of the Innocents will show how the playwright uses parody to offset the physical victory by the forces of evil. Like the slaughter, the scene is more formal than its analogues in the York, Chester, or *Ludus Coventriae* plays, and the language is liturgical in cast. In this highly stylized scene, there are three exchanges between the soldiers and Herod. In each, the three soldiers speak in turn and then the group is answered by Herod. When the soldiers leave, Herod addresses a hortatory soliloquy to the audience. The three *aves* marking the soldiers' departure suggest, in their similarity to the triple *sanctus* of the Mass, the reason for this structure: The scene, from the moment the soldiers turn toward Herod's court to the end of the play, is a parody of the Mass.

Herod's admonition to the audience opens and concludes with a promise of his imminent second coming. First he warns, "Wate when I com agayn / And then may ye craue" (467–68), and then he vows, "For if I here it spokyn when I com agayn / Youre branys bese brokyn" (505–6). In the Wakefield Ascension play, Christ's second coming is associated with his dispensing of reward and punishment:

> so com agane he shall,
> In the same manere at last ende,
> To deme both greatt and small.[44]

The Pauline source of the consecration connects this promised return with the Mass: "For as often as ye eat this bread, and drink this cup, ye do shew the Lord's death until he come" (I Cor. 11:26). Some medieval

versions of the Canon of the Mass include Herod's
words and remind us that the Mass is a continual anti-
cipation of the Second Coming: "As many times as
you shall do this, you shall do it in commemoration of
me, until I come again."[45] Since the figure of Herod
has already been endowed with the attributes of Antichrist, his promise of return denies the Second Coming. Throughout the play, Herod has forbidden men to
seek grace through the Mass:

> Lefe pystyls and grales;
> Mese, matyns noght avalys—
> All these I defende. (205–7)

The epistle of the Mass, proscribed by Herod, signifies
Christ's second coming: "The Epystyll ys a tokyn and
a fygure . . . / Of Crystys commyng by euydent scripture."[46] The naming of specific parts, like the gradual
and the epistle, as well as the whole, suggests that the
playwright has the Mass clearly in mind.

Not every detail of the parody Mass would be
noted, but because almost every word and thought in
the scene echoes the Mass as it was known in medieval
England, the audience would recognize in it a portrait
of the inverted system of prayer and reward involved
in the adoration of Herod as Antichrist. I have offered
a few possible stage directions to show how the playwright might have supported the verbal parallels with
the acting.

The playwright is not attempting to duplicate the
strict parallelism of the academic *Saufmessen,* but
rather to conceptualize the Mass in secular terms. For
example, the second half of Herod's warning, "and
then may ye crave," suggests a typical medieval attitude toward the Mass, i.e., of service rendered and
petition granted. The York *Lay Folks' Mass Book*
puts this in terms that could easily be secularized:

> þi merci, ihesu, wold I haue,
> and I for ferdnes durst hit craue
> bot þou bids aske, & we shal haue.[47]

Lydgate takes this further step and adds temporal success to the virtues of the Mass:

> Gase nat abowte . . .
> tyll tyme the preest haue do,
> Your good, your catall shall encrese yfeere.[48]

The parody Mass begins when the first soldier announces, "It syttys me to call my lord, as I wene" (408). The soldiers are seeking reward for their service of bloody sacrifice, and the decision to call upon Herod combines with their mutual admiration, "I shall say thou didst best— / Saue myself, as I gest" (411–12), to form an invitatory prayer[49] like this one from the York service: "Brothers and Sisters, pray for me as a sinner, so that likewise your sacrifice will be acceptable to the Lord God."[50] If we omit God from this prayer, a modified version of it would correspond to the soldiers' twisted belief that it is good to be the best sinner: "Put in a good word for me as a sinner, boys, so that both your sacrifice and mine will please our master." There is also in the soldier's "saue myself" a touch of that envious desire for precedence at the Mass which is found in the Wife of Bath and is condemned as a sign of boastful cowardice in the tracts of the age.[51]

The irony in the soldiers' mutual congratulation is brought out in the pun on "alow" as "lower" as well as "grant," which concludes their description of Herod as the *clementissime Pater* of the parodic *te igitur:* [53]

> Go furth now,
> Tell Herode oure tayll.
> For all oure avayll,
> I tell you, saunce fayll
> He wyll vs alow. (401–5)

The purpose of the gradual, which Herod has prohibited, is to uplift man: "Aftyr the epystyll foloweth the grayle, / Token of Ascending up from gre to gre."[54] If the soldiers believe in Herod they will descend to Hell, as the many references to Mahowne remind us.

Herod's confrontation with the soldiers, if its terms are taken on the wordly level of the participants in the scene, fits Gregory the Great's instructions for the consecration of the Mass, "Afterward the Gospel is read, then comes the offertory, and the petition over the offering is said."[55] The language of the greeting to Herod shows us how to make this translation. The address of the first soldier has a liturgical cast which fits Herod's usurpation of divine place. The request for Herod to listen, for example, is the standard "*domine exaudi*" that follows the introit in several medieval services:[56] "Hayll, Herode, our kyng. Full glad may ye be; / Good tythyng we bryng. Harken now to me" (415–16). The report of the slaughter is the gospel ("good tythyng") of Gregory's instruction, while the deed itself is the offering. The soldiers offer up a victim (*hostia*), only with the irony that they themselves have performed the slaughter. This offering is followed by the petition for reward, "Ye myght hold you well payde our lust to fulfyll" (436).

The offertory prayer found in every extant medieval liturgy summarizes much of the Mass and shows how the soldiers' offering of service and their request for monetary reward parodies valid prayer with its statement of religious service and hope for spiritual award: "We beg, O Lord, that thou and all thy household *will be pleased*, therefore, to accept this *offering of our service*: Dispose our days *in thy peace*, and *snatch us from eternal damnation*, and bid that we *be numbered* in the *flock of thy chosen ones*."[57] It has already been shown how the Slaughter of the Innocents is the offering of service; the three requests in the petition are each granted to the soldiers, although with an ironic twist. The desire for spiritual peace is mimicked by the political and emotional peace that Herod thinks he can give: "Now in peasse may I stand—I thank the, Mahowne!— / And gyf of my lande that longys to my crowne" (460–61). The second request for rescue from damnation receives its answer when Herod bids his soldiers to go "where [Mahowne] is lord freyndly" (459). Finally, Herod promises a bride for each soldier,

> Now by myghty Mahowne,
> ....
> Ye shall haue a lady
> Ilkon to hym layd, and wed at his wyll.
>   (429, 432–33)

The promise corresponds to the desire to be numbered among the flock of the elect. To emphasize the irony of these weddings, Herod soon enumerates the flock of Innocents whose slaughter will fulfill the number of the blessed as brides of the Lamb. With each of his blessings, it might be noted, Herod invokes the protection of Mahowne.

The soldiers' report is not only an offering; it is also confession, a prerequisite of the Mass. Each of the analogues to this play has only two soldiers, but the Wakefield version has three. This change allows the reports of the three soldiers to become a boastful parody of the three breast-beatings in the confession. As each soldier steps forward to announce his crime, he would probably point to his chest in pride. Thus in the three confessions of guilt we have a parody of *mea culpa, mea culpa,* and in the final claim to "no pyté," *mea maxima culpa.*[58] All this is rewarded by Herod "for now and evermore" (450), the words (*in saecula saeculorum*) used by the priest to conclude the Secret of the Mass.

After the Secret or Canon of the Mass was completed in the medieval English liturgy, the priest turned from his private devotion and elevated the host for the contemplation of the whole church. This public elevation explained to the general worshipers what had happened during the Canon, since the Canon had been said *secreto* or *submissa voce*.[59] In York, the public elevation was accompanied by a reminder of Christ's bloody sacrifice and a warning that disbelief would damn:

> And so þo leuacioun þou be-halde,
> for þat is he þat iudas salde, . . .
> and for mankynde þere shad his blode, . . .
> who trowes noght þis mone sitt ful myrk.[60]

The emphasis on the bloodiness of the sacrifice, a farsing of the consecration of the host ("This is the chalice of my blood . . . which was spilled for you and for many others in remission of sin"), was incorporated into the prayers said at this second elevation:

Hayle very bodye incarnate of a virgin
nayled on a crosse and offered for mannes synne,
whose syde beeyng persed, bloude ran oute plenteouslye.[61]

The Wakefield Master reproduces this part of the liturgy, which serves as the consecration of his parody Mass, when Herod turns to the audience from his private conference with the soldiers. The idea of elevation would be conveyed if Herod, who has probably been seated on a throne during the interview, were now to rise and move toward the audience. His boast about bloody victims is a twisted version of "this is my blood:"

> I sett by no good, now my hart is at easse,
> That I shed so mekyll blode. Pes, all my ryches!

> For to se this flode from the fote to the nese
> Mefys nothyng my mode. (469–72)

His attempt to gloss over his bloody deed and free himself from guilt ("my hart is at easse" and the following stanza on Herod's relief from despair)[62] would, in imitation of Pilate's handwashing,[63] constitute a parody of the priest's ablutions, performed after he receives offerings from the congregation but before the *sursum corda*.[64] We might speculate that during Herod's soliloquy the stage directions would indicate the use of some priestly gesture from the Mass or perhaps the ringing of a "sacring" bell as Herod tries to get the audience's attention.

Herod's final remarks include, as has been noted above, an earthly Pax, although it is absurdly a *pax mecum,* and a creed which denies the Creed:

> No kyng ye on call
> Bot on Herode the ryall,
> Or els many oone shal
> Apon youre bodys wonder. (501–4)

Such a denial was considered advocacy of the Antichrist: "And for asmoche as many toke vpon them to be called cryste, & wolde be called cryste of the people. as shall antecriste when he cometh. therfore to exclude that errour. & to shew that ther ys no cryste but one. the masse crede sayeth. *Et in vnum dominum iesum cristum.*"[65] Herod's anticreed and his promises of a second coming complete the parody Mass and fill out his role as Antichrist.

VI

Seen in the light of this parody, the scene provides a far more satisfying explanation of Herod's punishment than do the other English analogues. Paul the Deacon explains the major difficulty presented by the Slaughter of the Innocents: Why did Christ flee, leaving the children to suffer in his place? "Why did Christ, foreknowing what was to come, aware of those secrets, able to judge thoughts and read minds, desert those whom he knew would be sought on his account and murdered because of him?"[66] Such a question intrigues the playwright because it relates not only to this case, but also to the whole problem of the suffering of good men and their apparent desertion by Christ.

The Wakefield Master wants his audience to ask this question, and, by omitting the usual neat punishment of Herod, forces its prominence. In this way, the audience experiences the lack of satisfaction that comes when evil is unpunished and virtue is unrewarded. This experience comes even to the faithful who know the ultimate rightness of things. The other playwrights, who "solve" the problem of injustice by the immediate punishment of Herod, do not provide their audience with a way to deal with the injustices common in their daily life. The expectation of terrestrial retribution offered by the other plays can foster doubt when the audience finds that only on stage does evil receive its just deserts. Only when the immediate situation appears unjust must there be recourse to ultimate justice.

Parody accomplishes this reassertion by balancing the temporary triumph of evil with contrapuntal allusions to the eternal triumph of good. The greatest of these temporary disasters for good, Christ's own innocent sacrifice, is asserted in the Mass that appears through parody in the play. By continued contrast between the earthly and heavenly kings, the Wakefield Master requires his audience to reach the conclusion of Paul the Deacon: "Brethren, Christ did not look down upon his soldiers, but looked ahead; preferring to give them triumph rather than life, he made them seize victory without a struggle, gave them crowns rather than limbs, wished them to put by vices for virtues, and to possess heaven rather than earth."[67] Such an approach provides a deflationary view of sinister figures, while acknowledging that their power is temporarily frightening.

Herod's closing words are a final reminder of his inversion of all values and his denial of Christ. Like Chanticleer's "innocent" translation of *"mulier est hominis confusio,"* Herod's translation of *"adieu"* is deceptive. If one trusts Herod's French, he will end up where he is bid: "Bot adew!—to the deuyll! / I can no more Franch" (512–13).

VII • *Coliphizacio*
RENDING THE VEIL

While *Prima pastorum* illustrates the growth of the visionary imagination, *Coliphizacio* examines the opposite phenomenon, the progressive stages of spiritual blindness. The shepherds in the nativity play learn to see the unseeable, but the tormentors of the buffeting play cannot see or hear the Word even as it stands before them. Centuries before modern students of the media, our medieval playwright saw that awareness of any new medium must precede the understanding of its message. The Wakefield Master knew that the Incarnation was the most radical example of such a change of media—the Word was made flesh. Christ, as Incarnate Word, translates all the dead legalisms of the Old Testament into the living precepts of the New. Nothing can be read aright unless it is seen through Christ Incarnate. In the *Coliphizacio* the tormentors and the high priests reveal, in their continual demand that the Word speak, their inability to realize that His presence is itself the message He brings.

The Wakefield Master's dramatization of the buffeting is similar to the confrontation between a silent Christ and his ranting tormentors in the Chester version, but the Chester play does not exploit the contrast beyond keeping Christ silent through almost the entire play. This traditional contrast is set forth in a contemporary lyric:

> Then myn enmys begane to rage & rayle,
> And said I hade the devyll at my demayne;
> Some said I vsed arte magike wythought fayle,

And some said I coude not longe contynew ne rayne.
Al this I hard and litle I said a-gayne;
All that myne ennymes dyd I sufferd paciently,
And to the wordis no countraury speche hade I.[1]

The Wakefield Master seizes upon the paradoxical notion, only partially understood by the lyricist, that it is
this silence which speaks. The lyricist eventually mentions the Word—

The people I cured of euery maner sore . . .
Vsing to them noone other medycyne
But my holy worde, full of vertue divyne—[2]

but does not connect it to the notion of "no countraury speche."

To make the paradox of the silent Word contemporary, the Wakefield Master puts current legal language
into the mouths of Christ's oppressors and makes the
court ecclesiastical rather than Jewish. In this he
agrees with Rabanus Maurus, who finds that the incomprehension of the buffeters has passed from the
hands of the Jews and Romans: "The others, however, struck him in the face saying: 'Prophesy to us,
Christ, who it is that strikes Thee.' That man who was
then beaten by the buffets and blows of the Jews is
punished even now by the blasphemies of the false
Christians."[3] If the playwright's audience can hear the
answer of the silent Christ, then the play has taught
them to appreciate the change of media that is the
Incarnation. Once the play's objective is seen, there
remains the problem of why the playwright chose this
minor incident to present his vision of the Incarnate
Word.

In the first place, the action is appropriate to a symbolic presentation of the Word because the buffeting is
a type of the Crucifixion,[4] the event which separated
the Old Law from the New.[5] Those who do not com-

prehend the Incarnation cannot understand the change in the nature of human law which it caused: "But our sufficiency is of God: Who also hath made us able ministers of the New Testament; not of the letter but of the spirit; for the letter killeth, but the spirit giveth life" (2 Cor. 3:5–6). Christ's enemies, who do not know and cannot learn such distinctions, are blind to the Incarnation and its spiritual meaning. Instead, they soothe their discomfort in the alien presence of the Word by weaving numerous legalisms into a fabric of false reality that veils Christ and his mission from them.

The playwright also chooses the buffeting because he wants to accentuate Christ's unrivaled humility in taking on human flesh. Christ's immunity to the verbal buffets of his foes represents the self-control that manifests itself most magnificently in the Crucifixion. The Crucifixion cannot be substituted for the buffeting, however, because the play is figural, not allegorical. The meanings of the antitype are superimposed upon the different dramatic values of the type. Although the buffeting foreshadows the Crucifixion, it has none of its sublimity. The comic crudity of this punishment emphasizes how far Christ has humbled himself for mankind.

The very pettiness makes the indignity here greater than in the Crucifixion. Christ's hardest task in the buffeting is to suffer, not the pain, but the shame of such unworthy blows. Richard Rolle agrees with this interpretation: "I thanke þe, swete Lord Jhesu Cryst of þe pynus and of þe schamus þat þou suffryd before þe byschopus and maystres of þe lawe, and of þine enemys, of buffetys and of neckedyntes and of many other schames þat þou suffred."[6] The buffeting was seen as an absolute example of the humility of godhead assuming manhood—an epitome of the Incarnation: "In the buffeting and the spitting, every species of outrage was heaped upon him, so that he became the perfection of human humility."[7] Like Prometheus or Milton's Samson, Christ manifests his majesty, not so much through his physical suffering, as through his patient endurance of humiliation.

The Wakefield Master exercises tight control over the dramatic structure which encloses this symbolic content. As the silent Jesus moves through four confrontations with his mocking tormentors, his humiliation and his forbearance increase. The visible Word encounters, in turn, the boasting torturers, the raging Caiaphas, the subtle Annas, and finally the accumulated scorn of them all at the buffeting. Each of these *agons* furthers the definition of Christ's role as Word and extends our understanding of the myopia of his enemies. In this carefully structured succession of scenes, Christ's silence, unbroken except for one brief speech, endows him with awesome power.

II

Jesus' first confrontation is with the torturers, who counterpoint the silent agony of Christ's passion by filling the air with complaints more appropriate to their captive than to their own comfortable lives. The technique, similar to Herod's attribution of Christlike qualities to himself, emphasizes the figural value of the action since almost every word recalls some aspect of the passion. The torturers adopt, for example, the image of the transfixed heart which rightly belongs to Christ:

> It is wonder to dre, thus to be gangyng,
> We haue had for the mekill hart-stangyng;
> Bot at last shall we be out of hart-langyng. (10–12)

In the Crucifixion, the antitype of the buffeting, Christ undergoes "hart-stangyng" for all mankind: "þer he was wounded and vurst y-swunge, / With sharpe spere to herte y-stonge."[8]

The reversal of the roles of tormenter and sufferer continues as the first torturer complains to Caiaphas and Annas that no one cares about his weariness. Both Annas's response—"Say, were ye oght in dowte for fawte of light, / As ye wached therowte?" (55–56)—and the tormenter's report of the arrest recall Christ's agony in Gethsemane rather than any hardships of the tormenters:

> Of my dame sen I sowked had I neuer sich a nyght;
> My een were not lowked togeder right
> Sen morowe. (58–60)

The Wakefield audience knew that it was Christ whose eyes had not closed, since they had just seen the vigil in *The Conspiracy*, immediately preceding the *Coliphizacio*.

The torturer's accusation, "Thou has long had thi will, and made many brall" (29), further recalls the agony, since the audience had just seen Jesus forsake his own will in perfect obedience to his Father's. In Gethsemane, Christ had explicitly reminded his disciples of the power manifested in this play through his indomitable silence. Because of these echoes, the audience is aware of what Christ could do to these miserable boasters if he were following his will. The torturer's description of the capture attempts to denigrate the power exhibited in the Garden,

> Bot when I drew out my swerde,
> His dyscypyls wex ferde,
> And soyn they forsoke him. (70–72)

Yet *The Conspiracy* had dramatized the terror, not of Christ's followers, but of his captors, Malchus, for one, had panicked when Peter cut off his ear and returned to his bullying only when Jesus restored it. The torturer's boast about the night's swordplay alludes to Jesus' careful distinction between the Christian law of peace and the Roman law of the sword that was spelled out in the preceding play:

> Therfor, peter, I say the this,
> my will it is that all men witten:
> Put vp thi swerde and do no mys,
> for he that smytys, he shalbe smyten.[9]

The restraint imposed on Peter in the Garden has now become, in double measure, Christ's.

The transferred images of the agony in the Garden and of the Crucifixion also intensify the passivity of Christ's suffering. As the audience gradually recognizes that the torturers' complaints rightly belong to Christ, its rage becomes that of someone helplessly watching lying witnesses accuse an innocent defendant. The fact that Christ could respond to the torturers' audacious lies makes his restraint that much greater. The specific complaints made by the torturers also define Christ's role in the passion. Each complaint and accusation limns the shape of that awesome silence, just as every stroke of a pencil clarifies the image of a coin hidden behind a piece of paper.

The tormentors, however, remain deaf and blind to the visible Word. They do not see Christ; he has become an object, a chattel, as he is in the *Ludus Coventriae* version: "We payd to þi dyscyple for þe thretty pens / And as an ox or an hors we trewly þe bowth."[10] By driving Christ before them like an animal—"Do io furth, io! and trott on apase!" (1)—the torturers emphasize their own brutality and deny the double humanity necessary for salvation: their own as sinful creatures raised above the rest of creation, and Christ's as divinity descended to mankind.

In addition to showing how their vision of him is brutalized, the animal imagery is used by Christ's oppressors to place him outside the law. Caiaphas insists upon having "wols-hede and outhorne" (139) cried upon Christ. This traditional hue and cry reminds the audience that Christ, in the eyes of the blind Old Testament, is not only an animal but an outlaw.

The sense of outrage grows as the torturers blindly turn their ultimate judge into a criminal. A misplaced allusion to grace and eternal damnation intensifies the irony of the situation:

> Witt thou well: of thaym two gettys thou no grace,
> Bot euerlastyng wo, for trespast thou has
> So mekill. (3–5)

Christ's silence initiates the dramatic tension, as the listeners, who know the Sermon on the Mount—"ȝif ȝee shulen forȝeue to men her synnys, and ȝoure heuenly fadir shal forȝeue to ȝou ȝoure trespasses"—wait for a reply. Instead, Christ endures a tangle of legalisms ("ataynt," "legeance," "apeche," "forfet") and listens patiently as the torturers exalt what seems to them the supreme virtue of their law—its lack of mercy.

> For if other men ruse hym
> We shall accuse hym.
> Hisself shall not excuse hym,
> To you I insure it,
> With no legeance. (33–37)

As the torturers predict Caiaphas's and Annas's verdict, they further deny the hope that Christ brings: "Thi mys is more / Then euer gettys thou grace fore" (6–7). Since Christ does not respond to this belief in an unpardonable sin, the audience begins to defend him with his own, here unspoken, promises of endless grace for the greatest of misdeeds. As it is forced to recall the promises that filled the sermons and lyrics of the time, the audience is learning to hear the speech of silence.

The torturers, on the other hand, by dismissing Jesus' arguments beforehand, have forestalled any possibility of dialogue with him. From the beginning of the play, they have not really been talking to Jesus, but about him. This attitude becomes more noticeable as their references to Jesus drift from the second to the third person, as if he were not there—and for them, he is not. Up to the moment when they "tell of his talking," the torturers have defined Jesus as so much hot air—a man made of empty words: "fare wordys . . . many wordys . . . thi clatter." Since he is silent, they are not truly aware of his presence. As they constantly jibe him about his speaking, they ignore the Incarnation of the Word. To use Abelard's terminology, they are prepared to recognize him as "word" only in its most basic sense of sound, or movement of the air: "A striking of the air by the tongue, as witnesseth Boethius, is nonetheless a word."[11]

III

Jesus' second confrontation begins as the torturers hand him over to Caiaphas. The high priest does not ignore Jesus, as do his henchmen, but he cannot understand the significance of what Jesus is. He is willing to acknowledge Christ as "a sound which signifies,"[12] but not as a word which signifies or corresponds to reality. For Caiaphas, Jesus is much like the mythical *hircocervus* that Abelard is so fond of citing: "*Hircocervus* signifies something; . . . it is the name of a nonexistent thing."[13] Caiaphas listens to Christ's words, but can make no sense of them because his literalism cannot

interpret their spirit. For example, he cannot understand the spiritual meaning of resurrection in Christ's
words about the rebuilding of the temple:

> 2 TORTOR: Sir I hard hym say he cowthe dystroew oure
> tempyll so gay,
> And sithen beld a new on the thrid day.
> CAYPHAS: How myght that be trew? It toke more aray!
> The masons I knewe that hewed it, . . .
> That hewed ilka stone. (73–78)

Caiaphas's recollection of the stones hewed by each
mason recalls Paul's distinction between letter and
spirit, between words written on tablets of stone and
those written on the tablets of the heart (2 Cor. 3:3).
The ministration of death, not life, is figured with letters in stone. The accusations which follow Christ's
"lie" about rebuilding the temple show Christ as
healer and raiser of the dead, but the legalists can only
see in them deceit and black magic.

The petrified heart of pharisaical legalism is im-
aged forth in the accusations heaped upon Jesus in
Caiaphas's presence. Jesus, we are told, "lyes for the
quetstone" (80), but his "lies," in fact, recall his opposition to "stoniness." His accusers represent him as
a false lawyer who has, through his "soteltè," ex-
cused the woman taken in adultery. The woman, according to the Old Law, was to be stoned to death.
Christ's intervention, which said that no man should
cast the first stone, was part of the ministry of life.
His "antistoniness," a sign of resurrection, is attacked
as the legalists condemn his raising of Lazarus. The
Wakefield Master chooses this event as the final example of Christ's "lies" because his audience had just
seen Jesus in the *Lazarus* play roll back the stone
from over the grave.[14]

The image cluster of "stoniness" clarifies the
choice between pharisaical legalism and Christian

compassion that has already been established by the second torturer:

> Sich wyles can thou make,
> Gar the people farsake
> Our lawes, and thyne take;
> Thus art thou broght in blonder. (15–18)

The consistency with which Caiaphas and his minions maintain this foolish distinction allows them to misinterpret completely Christ's mission to "lege lawes new."

Caiaphas's failure to comprehend is symbolized in the irony of his attempt to force the Word, who has created all by his word, to say one word: "Though thi lyppis be stokyn, yit myght thou say 'mom,' / Great wordys has thou spokyn; then was thou not dom" (172–73). With the almost proverbial usage of "mom" in reference to tightfisted and closedmouthed lawyers, Caiaphas is suggesting that Jesus is a false advocate, like the one described in *Piers Plowman:*

> Seriauntes hij semed • that seruen atte barre,
> To plede for penyes • and poundes the lawe,
> And nat for loue of oure lord • vnlose hure lyppes ones.
> Thou myȝ bet mete the myst • on malverne hulles,
> Than get a mom of hure mouth • til moneye be hem shewid.[15]

Caiaphas converts Jesus into a wily mouthpiece whose eloquence defends lawbreakers. The pontifical court calls Jesus "a lord full renabyll" (11) who "lyfys bot bi brybré" (153), but Caiaphas hears nothing from him because he is awaiting the wrong kind of answer. Only at the end of the cycle, in the Judgment play, will sinners like Caiaphas learn that even a dozen lawyers bristling with legalisms cannot save them:

> Alas, I stande great aghe to loke on that Iustyce,
> Ther may no man of lagh help with no quantyce.

vokettys ten or twelfe may none help at this nede,
Bot ilk man for his self shall answere for his dede.[16]

Only then will the yelling torturers, who admonish
Christ "to halden still thy clatter," and the ranting
Caiaphas, who attempts to get him to "speke on oone
word," receive the answer that they now refuse to
hear.

In Caiaphas's nearly inarticulate rage, the Wakefield Master again demonstrates his interest in characters like Herod and Cain, whose fear emerges as
voluble madness. The weakness apparent in this rant
was traditionally contrasted with the might of Jesus'
silence: "How much braver was most benign Jesus in
being silent than was Caiaphas, who, overcome by
madness, tried to provoke him to answer with some
chance remark so that he might find grounds for an
accusation."[17]

Caiaphas reveals that Jesus has won the conflict for
domination that runs through the play:

> My hart is full cold, nerehand that I swelt.
> For talys that ar told I bolne at my belt—
> Vnethes may it hold my body, and ye it felt!
>
> (280–82)

Despite all the hot air which he has let loose, Caiaphas
is about to burst. His violent intentions fail to bring
about his aim of complete control of Jesus:

Sir Anna, all I wyte you this blame; for had ye not beyn,
I had mayde hym full tame—yei, stykyd hym, I weyn,
To the hart full wan with this dagger so keyn. (442–44)

IV

The third of Jesus' confrontations begins when Annas's crafty cross-examination replaces Caiaphas's rag-

ing soliloquy. The treatment of Annas is an innovation in dramatic technique. His "fair play" and measured, whispered words place far greater strain on Jesus' composure than the bombast of Caiaphas. Several other versions of the play contrast the two judges, but they do not exploit the innuendo of the Pharisee's role.

Annas, far more than Caiaphas, reveals the sinister nature of the Old Law.[18] Although Caiaphas always boasts about his authority, he can never control the situation. When he strikes at Christ and misses, Annas coolly points out the reason: "Ye ar irregulere" (306), that is, out of the rules. Annas works only as the law allows, but he thinks that this will be enough. "All soft may men go far; oure lawes ar not myrk" (211). With a sinister smile he says,

> *Et hoc nos volumus*
> *Quod de jure possumus*
> Ye wote what I meyn—
> It is best that we trete hym with farenes. (214–17)

He, not the blustering Caiaphas, arranges the buffeting. Caiaphas cannot understand Christ's spiritual message, but since he would operate outside the law, he cannot represent its alternative. Annas, on the other hand, by his devotion to the letter of the law destroys its spirit. Compared to Annas's subtlety, Caiaphas's external threats pose little danger to Christ's position.

The wily Annas commands a full arsenal of indirect legal strategy. His danger lies in the fact that he seems to offer an honorable retreat. He will not force Jesus into a corner, and even after Jesus acknowledges his rightful place, Annas counsels calm: "Was ther neuer man so wyk bot he myght amende / When it com to the pryk, right as youreself kend" (262–63). Annas does not argue about Christ's guilt; he assumes it.

Annas's incomprehension of Christ's mission is as subtle as his strategy. Caiaphas's more opaque blindness can only see a rival king in worldly terms:

> What, nawder bowted ne spurd and a lord of name? . . .
> Perdé, if thou were a kyng,
> Yit myght thou be ridyng. (147, 150–51)

Annas, on the other hand, tries to circumscribe Jesus with the law. He intends to discredit Jesus' way as an alternative by showing not only that Christ is outside the law but also that the Old Testament law is reasonable and gentle. Hence he warns Caiaphas to imitate the mildness that is Christ's hallmark: "Sir, thynk ye that ye ar a man of holy kirk; / Ye shuld be oure techere, mekenes to wyrk" (208–9). Caiaphas's part in the buffeting, of course, reveals the depth of this meekness.

Jesus' silence avoids the entanglements of the law. His refusal to deny Annas's claims to mercy and mildness shows greater self-restraint than his ability to ignore Caiaphas's bluster. The silence traditionally marks both condescension and humility: "Jesus, however, was silent, seeing that it would be unworthy to answer him according to the prophecy: 'While the sinner stood against me, I was silent, I was greatly humbled, and I did not speak for good reason.' "[19] Just as significantly, the silence reveals his enemy's inability to see him or his purpose. Annas's question, which elicits the only words spoken by Jesus, offers a way to escape crucifixion through the denial of the Incarnation:

> Why standys thou so styll when men thus accuse the?
> For to hyng on a hyll, hark how thay ruse the
> To dam.
> Say art thou Godys son of heuen,
> As thou art wonte for to neuen. (246–50)

Jesus' reply returns Annas's own words to show that
Annas does not know—or rather, does not believe—
what he has said. The truth has been in front of his
eyes, but he has not seen it: "So thou says by thy
steuen, / And right so I am" (251–52). This culminates
the words about words emphasizing the court's refusal
to listen to any of Christ's words because it has not
seen him. Annas represents the third stage of the tormentors' failure to recognize the Word. Christ is seen
by Annas as *verbum,* "for a sound does not in any way
naturally belong to a thing signified, except as it is
imposed by man,"[20] not *Verbum.* Just as a word is
given signification by man, so Annas believes Christ's
name is a word that is not part of his essence. Seen
this way, Christ's law is only a local truth based upon
his opinions, not a universal truth that can invalidate
the laws by which Annas lives. Unlike Caiaphas or the
torturers, Annas understands Christ's role but refuses
to believe it: the ultimate misunderstanding.

V

These three confrontations prepare us for the final
agon in which all three opponents—the torturers,
Caiaphas, and Annas—join to heap humiliation upon
Christ. In this they are led by the clown-Garcio figure, Froward, whose name suggests "one who turns
his back"[21] and who represents all the kinds of deaf-
ness and blindness that have been presented to this
point. In the Wakefield *Crucifixion,* the torturers
mock Christ by calling the Cross the saddle upon
which he must ride to the tournament of his Crucifixion. The Wakefield Master superimposes the game
aspect of this mockery upon the straightforward brutality of the York version of the buffeting to produce

a mock Crucifixion that outdoes the indignity of the latter event.

The "vayll" that Christ wears is an ironic reminder of the veil that covers the hearts of those who cannot see beyond the Old Testament. Special attention is paid to the "vayll." It is mentioned twice, and Froward makes a special trip to get it. He looks upon it from the Old Testament view, "Here a vayll haue I fon; I trow it will last" (388). Paul's comment on the spirit of the New Law explains the folly of Froward's expectation: "But til in to this day, whanne Moyses is radd, the veyl is putt vpon her hertis. Forsoth whanne Israel schal be convertid to God, the veyl schal be don awey" (2 Cor. 3:16–17). In *The Resurrection of the Lord,* the Wakefield audience will hear the centurion report to Caiaphas that the veil in the temple has been torn:

> Not oonly for the son wex myrke,
> Bot how the vayll rofe in the kyrke,
> ffayn wyt I wold.[22]

Rabanus Maurus, among other commentators, has identified the veil used in the buffeting as the veil which blinds those who see only by the half-light of the Old Testament:

For they veiled his face, as Mark tells us the Jews did then; not so he might not see their crimes, but as the Old Testament says, so they might hide themselves from the benefit of recognizing him. For if they had believed Moses, perhaps they would have believed the Lord. For even today, that veil remains unlifted from their hearts, but it has been removed from those of us who believe in Christ. For not in vain was the veil of the temple rent in two at his death, and those things which were hidden during the entire reign of the Law, and concealed from fleshly Israel, those holy secrets of secrets were made known to the believers in the New Testament.[23]

The veil symbolizes the blindness of the legalists of the Old Testament and parodies the transfer of guilt which occurs in the Crucifixion. As Jesus will take up the sins of man, who crucifies him, so here he assumes the blindness of those who buffet him.

A second symbolic motif in the veiling of Christ extends the implied condemnation of his tormentors' folly. In the game of hot cockles, the blindfolded Christ must judge who was the last to strike him and point out the culprit.[24] In the legal framework of the play, the game suggests that the blindfolding of Christ represents Froward's foolish attempt to obscure true justice. Erwin Panofsky points out that blindfolded Justice was not a sign of legal equality until the sixteenth century, but earlier, "in Sebastian Brant's *Narrenschiff*, [for example,] the fool still bandages the eyes of Justice in order to defeat her true purpose."[25] This attempt to veil the truth and to break Christ's will proves as fruitless as the ultimate folly of the Crucifixion.

To be fully effective as a precursory action, the buffeting must include specific allusions to the Crucifixion. These are elaborated about the central image of the veil. As in the Crucifixion, Jesus is made a mock king, "Therfor I shall the name . . . / King Copyn in oure game" (165–66). Elaborately dressed, most probably like a prince of fools, Christ is given a throne; "lyke a lord of renowne youre sete is arayde" (362). In the *Fflagellacio,* Christ has to bear his own cross to Calvary.[26] Froward converts the stool into a symbolic Cross by forcing Christ to carry it, foreshadowing the later burden. The crown of thorns, together with the mocking inscription on the Cross, "ihesu of nazareyn he is kyng of Iues,"[27] is alluded to in the torturer's remark, "We shall preue on his crowne the wordys he has sayde" (363). The blows of the buffeting are meant to be felt like the nails on the Cross, "Godys forbot ye lefe, bot set in your nalys / On raw" (409–10). This will echo in the minds of the audience when they hear the torturers nail Christ to the Cross in *The Crucifixion:*

> Do dryfe a nayll ther thrugh outt,
> And then thar vs nothyng doutt,
> for it will not brest.[28]

The torturers' request during the buffeting that the blindfolded Christ tell them who has smitten him becomes like the mocking request at the Crucifixion for Christ to come down if he can.[29] In both cases the audience knows that Christ can do exactly what is asked of him and does not have to undergo this torment except to become the Salvation.

After the mock Crucifixion, Caiaphas sends Christ to Pilate for judgment, which will constitute the final act of justice under the Old Law. Pilate has several times been referred to as a "temperall" judge. Annas means to contrast Pilate with himself in his ecclesiastical office, but the real contrast is with the spiritual judgment of Christ. Three legal spheres operate in this play—those presided over by Pilate, Caiaphas, and Christ. The first two are merely aspects of the Old Law, while only Christ governs the New. Pilate's court is not the proper place for the judgment of Christ, "for he is a iuge sett emang men of state" (426).

The New Law brings with it the proscription, "judge not, that ye be not judged" (Matt. 7:1). This condemns the folly of all those in this play who attempt to judge the actions of Christ by the Old Law. His only speech, which is placed near the center of the play, reminds his judges that he will not be so passive in his second coming. This is an allusion to the Last Judgment, the final act of justice under the New Law: "For after this shall thou se when that I do com downe / In brightnes on he, in clowdys from abone" (153–54). The *Ludus Coventriae* makes explicit the warning in Christ's words:

> Goddys sone I am I sey not nay to þe
> And þat ȝe all xall se At domys-day
> Whan þe sone xal come • in gret powere and majeste
> And deme þe qweke and dede as I þe say.[30]

This is a warning to recognize the Incarnation now, for there will be no blindness on the Day of the Judgment. Rather, the sinners will wonder how to avoid seeing him then:

> How may I on hym loke,
> That falsly hym forsoke,
> When I led synfull lyfe?[31]

The legalistic priestly class, represented especially by Annas, feels that it can afford to ignore the warning of the Judgment because it believes that time will always continue under its law. Such men, through their reliance on the written word, are bound to reason and causality, both of which seem to preclude the abolition of time. Eventually law, a word which Annas uses constantly, comes to justify not only his accusations, but his version of reality itself.

In the *Coliphizacio* the oppressors' confused reaction to Christ comes from their dependence upon sequential logic. From Caiaphas's misinterpretation of the rebuilding of the temple, to the absurdity of the King of the World allowing himself to be "it" in a game of hot cockles, to the final promise of a judgment beyond time, nothing Christ does or says follows the reason or logic that the literalists expect. The Wakefield playwright continually uses imagery and phrasing to point out this blindness. During the climactic game of hot cockles, when Froward, in the tones of John of Patmos, says, "I stod and behold" (400), he most excruciatingly misses the point. Froward beholds only that his fellows have not struck hard enough, where the whole weight of the play suggests that the man with symbolic vision would perceive the humility that will reach fruition on the Cross.

Christ's tormentors recognize him as Word on three levels, none of which corresponds to the truth. The torturers see him simply as a vibration in the air, a noise, and do not listen to him at all. Caiaphas listens and finds the Word incomprehensible nonsense, like the centaur or *hircocervus*. Annas, on the other hand, knows what Jesus means, but denies its validity, since the Word works by a logic alien to his own. For Annas, Jesus as Word is a lie, which, were it truth, would destroy his system of values. Not one of them understands that with the Incarnation, Word takes on a new meaning, since it becomes the new reality.

VIII · Symbolic Action
SOME ANALOGUES IN ART AND DRAMA

"Iste perfecit opus." Fra Lippo Lippi, as Browning reveals, includes his humble worldly self in a work of great spiritual significance, and his presence suggests a distinctive quality of the Wakefield Master as a late medieval artist. Just as Lippo's masterpiece, by portraying the relation of a sinner like himself to the divine, surpasses strictly hagiographical subjects on one hand and charcoals direct from life on the other, so the Wakefield playwright, by placing the contemporary world of his fellow townsmen on the larger canvas of spiritual absolutes, transcends the separate genres of secular and religious drama.

The early critical emphasis on realistic elements in the plays derives from a kind of cultural Darwinism which makes medieval drama an ungainly ape waiting to evolve into its Shakespearean manhood. O. B. Hardison points out that the approach of E. K. Chambers or Karl Young makes it impossible for either of them to regard the medieval stage in and of itself: "That it remained teleological is indicated by Chambers's preface, in which the final goal of the work is defined as 'to state and explain the preexisting conditions which, by the latter half of the sixteenth century, made the great Shakespearean stage possible.' "[1] Because of this viewpoint, Chambers finds the drama about to emerge from the Middle Ages good only in its realism. "The view encouraged by *The Medieval Stage* is that drama originated in spite of Christianity, not because of it."[2] Both Hardin Craig and Eleanor Prosser react against this realistic bias in criticism of the drama, and a pendulum swing brings them to the opposite side: Only the religious element is worthwhile in medieval drama. Each of these extreme views devalues half of the genius of the Wakefield Master.

In his unique vision, the Wakefield Master perceives the analogous temporal and eternal worlds as interacting in such a way that each helps interpret the other. Two painters of this period, Bosch and Bruegel, give graphic examples of the kind of insights that might be expected from contemporary audiences. A triptych by Bosch suggests how a realistic object might unfold its symbolic significance to a medieval viewer. A triptych consists of three panels: a central one, and two, half its size, which are painted front and back. The side panels close over the central one, hiding all three inner panels. The closed triptych most often composes one picture, although sometimes each panel forms a separate scene. Bosch's scheme for the revelation of the three inner panels of the triptych can help teach one how to read the parodied scenes in the Wakefield plays.

In one example, the outside of the wing panel presents a child carrying a paper windmill in one hand and holding a walking frame in the other. When the triptych is opened, the viewer discovers a scene of Christ carrying the Cross and understands that the child is Christ and the toy windmill stands for the Cross he is to bear. One of Bosch's critics explains why one must not recognize the infant as Christ until the triptych is opened: "What is new is the human way in which Bosch tells the tragic tale. . . . In the idea of presenting a confessor next to one of the thieves, an innovation that Bruegel was to adopt, Bosch seems to have wanted to link the Biblical event with his own times, and this may also be why he depicted himself as a witness of the scene. The entire conception seems to lay bare the human situation that is expressed in the popular saying, 'we have each our cross to bear.' "[3] The Wakefield Master uses the revelation of symbolic resonance similarly. The sheep-hiding scene in Mak's cottage only becomes significant as a parody of the Nativity when one sees the real Nativity and appreciates the parallel. As with Bosch, the audience must understand how its humanity fits into both scenes.

In Bosch's work, and even more in that of his follower Bruegel, there are numerous similarities to the Wakefield Master in manner of representation, in theme, and in symbolic conception. To find, for example, how the Wakefield Master envisions the tormentors in his plays, one need only look at the faces in several depictions of the Procession to Calvary by both painters. All three artists see that half-human brutality so familiar to nations at war. Such insight into mankind's attitudes creates a dramatic, three-dimensional realism that is used to present the same basic theme— the juxtaposition of contemporary folly and inhumanity with the biblical world of Christ. This concern has led the Dutch painters, as well as the English playwright, to dramatize current proverbs and sayings as commentary on the *imitatio Christi*. The contemporaneity of scene helps to relate the audience directly to Christ. De Tolnay notes how Bosch involves the spectator in the painting, much as the Wakefield Master does when he has Garcio remind the audience that some of them are Cain's men. In the depiction of Christ carrying the Cross, "a cross of unusual size weighs heavily upon the Saviour, and yet it is not this burden which afflicts Him. His questioning gaze is directed towards the spectator and calls him to account for his association with the executioners and traitors.

These become the principal actors in the drama, in which the spectator, identified with them, takes part directly."[4] This process of spectator involvement is also a basic didactic tool of the Wakefield playwright.

Bruegel presents an even closer parallel to the symbolic imagination of the Wakefield Master. The Wakefield Master's ability to turn the apparently marginal presence of Christ into the symbolic center of his drama has been noted several times. In the *Coliphizacio,* for example, Christ is virtually silent for the whole play, and in the *Magnus Herodes* his presence is felt only through allusion and parody, yet this presence ultimately dominates each play. Bruegel parallels this technique, for unlike earlier painters, he will put Christ in a scene without making him the pictorial focus. In the two paintings that will now be examined, *Netherlandish Proverbs* and *The Procession to Calvary,* one has to search for the figure of Christ, but once he is recognized, it becomes clear that the intricate symbolism of each painting revolves about his presence.

Bruegel's encyclopedic *Netherlandish Proverbs* illustrates every imaginable example of human folly, particularly the hyperliteral kind found in the *Prima pastorum.* The subject matter of the painting takes the viewer immediately into the imaginative world of the Wakefield Master. There are numerous examples of the worldly anality of *Mactacio Abel,* the uxoriousness of the *Secunda pastorum,* and, in the center, we see Noah's wife's expression, "Thou were worthi be cled in Stafford blew," dramatized. The whole of the painting recalls the elaboration of the proverbial tale of the three Fools of Gotham in the *Prima pastorum.* As in the *Prima pastorum,* folly is dressed in contemporary guise, but in the midst of this sixteenth-century Dutch worldliness, one finds Christ, almost hidden by the myriad figures. He sits with one hand on the orb, giving his blessing to one of the fools. The appearance of this anachronistic figure is similar to the sudden break in the time scheme at the end of the *Prima pastorum,* which transforms the worldly fools into prophetic fools for Christ. Furthermore, Bruegel symbolically suggests that this world is an inversion of Christ's by repeating the motif of the orb throughout the painting: a juggler uses one for his act to illustrate the proverb, "he lets the world dance on his thumb";[5] an orb is used for belling the cat; the fool crawls into a surrealistically egglike orb; and finally, an inverted orb is used for a tavern sign. This use of a leitmotif to comment contrapuntally on human folly is also found in the *Prima pastorum,* where the motif of Mowll and her one eternal sheep is repeated in the argument over nonexistent sheep, in Garcio's remark about the surrealistic appearance of midwinter pasturage for suddenly real sheep, and finally in the reference to Christ as Lamb. The orb with its cross parallels the sheep/lamb in its duality of symbolism, since both can stand either for worldliness or for Christ's dominion in the world. As has been shown in the chapter on this play, the Wakefield Master would clearly understand Bruegel's contention that the folly of the world stems largely from the literalism that makes it impossible for the worldly to see Christ in their midst.

Bruegel's handling of a biblical scene in *The Procession to Calvary* further illustrates the similarity between his symbolic technique and that of the Wakefield Master. At first glance, the canvas seems to be a realistic portrayal of the scene in the anachronistic terms of a contemporary execution. One has to search for Christ amid a swarm of indifferent humanity and discovers that Bruegel contrasts Christ's suffering and the brutality of his tormentors, much as the Wakefield Master

does in the *Coliphizacio*. A further examination of the
realistic surface of the painting reveals that it is charged
with symbolic overtones.

The procession moves from left to right. Nature undergoes a symbolic transformation as the eye follows
the movement toward the right, losing "all her verdant
splendor as the crowd moves on toward the bleak
desolation of the fatal hill."[6] On the left side of the
picture the trees are green and the sky is midday blue,
but toward Calvary, the landscape becomes brown and
bare and the sky is gradually covered by darkening
storm clouds. A budding tree and a young lamb on the
left give place to a treelike torture pole and a cow's
skull on the right. This symbolic use of weather and
landscape is similar to the Wakefield Master's treatment of these elements in both shepherds' plays.
Neither artist comments overtly on the symbolism, but
the atmosphere in each case provides the proper mood
for the audience's reaction to events.

Beyond this similarity of symbolic atmosphere,
Bruegel's painting presents an analogue to one of the
most distinctive features of the Wakefield Master's
art—the sudden transformation of contemporary time
into biblical timelessness—a phenomenon which occurs
at the end of both shepherds' plays and in the reverse
order at the beginning of the Noah play. In the fore-
ground of *The Procession to Calvary* stand four saintly
mourners who are clearly of a different order from the
hundreds of people on their way to celebrate the execution. Gustav Glück explains how Bruegel sets the
mourners off from the remainder of the painting's
world: "These figures have nothing of the realistic form
of the others; they appear, with their elongated propor-
tions and their timelessly conceived dress, to be each a
type. Bruegel, as we have seen, has designated this
formulation for his ideal-figures."[7] By placing Christ in

the realistic portion of the picture while maintaining his relation to these timeless figures, Bruegel makes us aware of Christ's duality as man and God. Like the Wakefield Master, Bruegel wants to capture the human drama of Christ's descent into this world, while never ignoring his separation from it.

Like Bruegel, the Wakefield Master requires the viewer to appreciate the differing styles within his work. It might be well to speculate, therefore, upon the way in which the Wakefield audience would react to the procession of pageant wagons that present the *cursus mundi*—the entire history of the world.

Despite whatever typological knowledge he had absorbed from sermons, books, or the church-as-book, the viewer would react initially to the characters of these plays as human beings who dress and speak very much as he does. The effect of the pageant wagons upon the mind of the spectator must have been incremental rather than instantly typological. The first reaction to Noah's wife is not that she is a type of Eve, but that she is a shrew, just like my wife, who has been nagging me all morning to fix the leaky roof. Once this level is reached, the spectator will begin to notice the verbal and scenic keys that suggest the connection to Eve. The art of the Wakefield Master works particularly well here because of the vitality of its realistic surface. The attention of critics in the early part of this century to this realism typifies what must have been the first reaction to his plays. In conjunction with the allegorical level, the realism causes the ambivalence of the playwright's symbols. This ambivalence prevents the figures on stage from ever becoming simply types and so contributes to the Master's humanity.

The audience will come to connect Cain with the Jews as the slayer of Christ, but they can never forget how like them he is both in his difficulties in getting his farming done and as a man capable of anger. The "coolness," in Marshall McLuhan's terms, of the symbolic medium forces the audience to react with both fear and sympathy. Had the playwright presented him allegorically as Cain, who, like the vile Jew, slew our Lord, no sense of the terror of Cain's situation could be evoked; he would simply become the object of hate.

The progression of the wagons also works to this effect because the audience only gradually understands that all of the human events prefigure the life of Christ. Because of the annual occurrence of the plays, there would be some sense throughout the cycle of what was to come, but only the ultimate appearance on stage could confirm this in the minds of the audience.

Although Kolve is right in contending that "plays called Corpus Christi imitate all time, in chronological sequence and as metaphysical structure, achieving instead of the expressive point of the French and Cornish pattern a formal completeness almost sacramental in its impact,"[8] one must also realize that this awareness comes only after the cycle has been completed. To understand how these plays would affect a medieval audience, one must consider the effect caused by the appearance of a succession of stage wagons like those described by Wickham.[9] Unlike the microcosmic effect of the theatre in the round as it is described by Southern,[10] the playgoer's initial attitude is not one of facing an allegorical representative of Mankind, but a specific individual.

Often a particular stage design reflects a world view. Ibsen's claustrophobic sets, for example, suggest a world cut off from God and nature but not particularly concerned with this excision. The characters seem concerned only with their own frustrated social interaction. Bringing the forest into the house in *The*

Wild Duck is an extreme example, but the stage set for *Hedda Gabler* is equally stifling. In each case there seems to be nothing outside, and what is more pathetic, the characters have ceased to worry about this loss. Beckett, on the other hand, by the sense of infinite emptiness surrounding the characters in the sets of *Waiting for Godot* or *Endgame,* shows that his primary concern is with this emptiness—all that really matters is the nothing that is out there.

The peculiar staging of the cyclical drama also creates a certain world view. The appearance of a succession of pageant wagons would first impress the audience with a sense of particularity and temporality, since both the playing area and the time for the performance of each individual play are limited. The contemporary costumes clothing the biblical figures would add to this sense of action in time, as would the realistic dialogue dealing with contemporary issues. As each wagon is superimposed upon the spot that the preceding one left, however, and as a *sedes* or piece of stage machinery acquires second and third meanings, a new sense of simultaneity would emerge. Thus, when the audience becomes sensible that the same hill is Christ's tomb and the Mount of Calvary a new attitude of timelessness will be acquired. If, as Stanely Kahrl suggests, the pageant wagons formed a series of *tableaux vivants* as they moved between stations, this response would be reinforced.[11] During any one play the awareness of change would be negligible, but as the sun sets over the last play of the day, the spectator must feel the contemporaneity of all time. Kolve's chapter on this latter sensation shows how effective this was as a didactic device, but does not quite capture the double sense of time and timelessness, of human being and type which is peculiar to the Wakefield Master.[12]

The playwright, through symbolic action, gives value to man's individual acts as a means of relating to the divine: Oswald the fishmonger is suddenly able to act, as Noah, both like the henpecked husband that he is and at the same time like the creator who made him. Thus the actor becomes a symbol of man, created in the image of his maker, who in this fallen world remains at an infinite distance from him.

Notes

I • *The Wakefield Master*

1. Alfred W. Pollard, intro., *The Towneley Plays*, ed. George England, p. xxviii.

2. The first pages of the Wakefield *Judgment* are missing, but since we have the complete York play, the Master was not patching an incomplete play.

3. V. A. Kolve, *The Play Called Corpus Christi*, pp. 57–100.

4. Pollard, in England, *The Towneley Plays*, xxii.

5. Pollard, in England, *The Towneley Plays;* A. C. Cawley, *The Wakefield Pageants in the Towneley Cycle;* and Rosemary Woolf, *The English Mystery Plays* agree on the attribution of the play to the Wakefield Master. Arnold Williams, *The Drama of Medieval England*, disagrees.

6. Walter E. Meyers, *A Figure Given*, p. 43.

7. Woolf, *Mystery Plays*, p. 251.

8. Carl Linfert, *Hieronymus Bosch*, p. 88.

9. Ibid., p. 90.

10. England, *The Towneley Plays*, p. 376.

11. Ibid., p. 377.

12. Ibid.

13. Woolf, *Mystery Plays*, p. 304.

14. Bob Claessens and Jeanne Rousseau, *Our Brueghel*, pl. 46n.

15. Millicent Carey, *The Wakefield Group in the Towneley Cycle*, p. 241.

16. J. W. Robinson, "The Art of the York Realist," p. 244.

17. Kolve, *Corpus Christi*, pp. 8–32.

18. Martin Stevens, "Illusion and Reality in the Medieval Drama," pp. 448–64.

19. Ibid., p. 457.

20. Eleanor Prosser, *Drama and Religion in the English Mystery Plays*, p. 187.

21. Charles Gayley, *Plays of Our Forefathers*.

22. F. M. Salter, *Mediaeval Drama in Chester*, p. 84.

23. Prosser, *Drama and Religion*, p. 81.

24. Williams, *Drama*, p. 129.

25. Ibid., p. 128.

26. J. A. Schmeller, ed., *Carmina Burana*, p. 20:

> Numus est pro numine
> et pro Marco marca
> et est minus celebris
> ara quam sit arca.

27. Ibid., p. 72:

> Venter deus meus erit,
> talem deum gula quaerit,
> cuius templum est coquina
> in qua redolent divina, . . .
> cuius mensa et cratera
> sunt beatitudo vera.

28. Augustine, *La Trinité*, 16:184. "Nam et animae in ipsis peccatis suis non nisi quamdam similitudinem Dei, superba et praepostera, et ut ita dicam, servili libertate sectantur. Ita nec primis parentibus nostris persuaderi peccatum posset, nisi diceretur, 'Eritis sicut dii.' "

29. *Les Confessions*, 8:354 (Bk. 2, ch. 6). "Perverse te imitantur omnes, qui longe se a te faciunt et extollunt se adversum te, sed etiam sic te imitando indicant creatorem te esse omnis naturae."

30. Ibid. "Nam et superbia celsitudinem imitatur, cum tu sis unus super omnis deus excelsus. . . . Et saevitia potestatem timeri vult: quis autem timendum nisi unus deus."

31. *La Trinité*, 16:184. "In quantum ergo bonum est quidquid est, in tantum scilicet, quamvis longe distantem, habet tamen nonnullam similitudinem summi boni, et si naturalem, utique rectam et ordinatam; si autem vitiosam utique turpem utque perversam."

32. One must note that parody in the Augustinian sense does not criticize the action or work parodied but the parody itself. This distinction must be emphasized because the term *parody* has caused consternation among some critics of the Wakefield Master. E. K. Chambers, *English Literature*

at the Close of the Middle Ages (p. 38), is disturbed by the parody nativity in *The Second Shepherds' Play* because he sees it as a degradation of the true Nativity. To someone approaching the term *parody* from, let us say, Byron's parodies of Shelley or Wordsworth, this would seem to be the case, for here the criticism is aimed at the object of parody rather than the parody itself. *Mac Flecknoe* exemplifies the second type, in which the satirical adversaries are Flecknoe and Shadwell, not the Baptist and his Lord.

33. Francis Thompson, "Unity in *The Second Shepherds' Tale*" pp. 302–6, and William Manley, "Shepherds and Prophets: Religious Unity in the Towneley *Secunda pastorum*," pp. 151–55, exemplify this tendency. John Gardner, "Imagery and Illusion in the Wakefield Noah Play," pp. 3–12, has dealt successfully with the comic tone of allegorized action.

34. Erich Auerbach, *Scenes from the Drama of European Literature,* p. 53.

35. Ibid., p. 27.

36. Kolve, *Corpus Christi,* passim.

37. Charles Singleton, "Dante's Allegory," p. 80.

38. Ibid.

39. Arnold Williams, "Typology and the Cycle Plays: Some Criteria," p. 680.

40. R. E. Kaske, in Dorothy Bethurum, ed., *Critical Approaches to Medieval Literature,* p. 27.

41. G. R. Owst, *Literature and Pulpit in Medieval England;* M. D. Anderson, *Drama and Imagery in English Medieval Churches.*

42. Morton Bloomfield, "Symbolism in Medieval Literature," p. 76.

II • Cain's Foul Wrath

1. Wisdom 11:17.

2. John Gardner, "Theme and Irony in the Wakefield *Mactacio Abel,*" p. 519.

3. All quotations from the six plays are in A. C. Cawley, ed., *The Wakefield Pageants in the Towneley Cycle.*

4. Cain complains that with the growth of mankind, "chacun se vouldra dire maistre / Et se donner auctorité." James de Rothschild, ed., *Le Mistère du Viel Testament*, 1:80.

5. Augustine, *De civitate Dei, PL*, 41.444. "Et hoc est proprium terrenae civitatis, Deum vel deos colere, quibus adjuvantibus regnet in victoriis et pace terrena, non charitate consulendi, sed dominandi cupiditate."

6. Hermann Deimling, ed., *The Chester Plays*, 1:43.

7. Augustine, *De civitate Dei, PL*, 41.460. "Cain quippe genuit Enoch, in cujus nomine condidit civitatem, terrenam scilicet, non peregrinantem in hoc mundo, sed in ejus temporali pace ac felicitate quiescentem."

8. Canto 15, translated by John Ciardi.

9. Prosser, *Drama and Religion*, p. 76.

10. Mary Macleod Banks, ed., *An Alphabet of Tales*, 1:43.

11. Hugh of Saint Victor, *Adnotationes elucidatorie in Pentateuchon, PL*, 175.44. " 'In Cain signum,' id est tremorem membrorum quasi fanatici, id est furibundi."

12. "Piped so small" almost directly translates the Vulgate's "sibilum tenuis aurae" from the story of Elijah on Mount Horeb (1 Kings 19:12).

13. Ambrose, *De poenitentia, PL*, 17.1064. "Nescio, numquid custos fratris mei sum ego? 'O insaniam detestabilem!' "

14. John D. Sinclair, ed., *Dante's Purgaturio*, 14.133: "Anciderammi qualunque m'apprende."

15. Ibid., 15.61–63.

> Com'esser puote ch' un ben distributo
>   in più posseditor faccia più ricchi
> di sè che se da pochi è posseduto?

16. Deimling, *The Chester Plays*, 1:42.

17. The Vulgate has "*maxilla*" but as early as 1380, Wycliffe translates the word as "cheek:" "But I seie to ʒou that ʒe aʒenstonde not an yuel man, but if ony man smyte thee in the riʒt cheke: schewe to hym tother."

18. Anderson, *Drama and Imagery*, p. 26.

19. Prosser, *Drama and Religion*, p. 78.

20. Sinclair, *Dante's Inferno,* 22.1–12.

21. F. N. Robinson, ed., *The Works of Geoffrey Chaucer,* Summoner's Tale, ll. 1689–91. All subsequent citations are to this edition.

22. For the Goliards, the sulphurous smell of Rome warns visitors that the spiritual city has become the city of Antichrist:

> Roma caput mundi est, . . .
> trahit enim vitium . . .
> et de fundo redolet
> quod est juxta fundum.

Schmeller, *Carmina Burana,* p. 19.

23. K. S. Block, ed., *Ludus Coventriae,* p. 29.

24. Deimling, *The Chester Plays,* 1:41.

25. Chaucer, Summoner's Tale, ll. 1967–69.

26. J. E. Whitesell, "Chaucer's Lisping Friar," pp. 160–61.

27. Chaucer, Summoner's Tale, ll. 2147–49.

28. Jerome, *Commentarii in Epistolas B. Pauli, PL,* 30.873. "Suavissimus Deo odor est charitas."

29. Ambrose, *De Cain et Abel, PL,* 14.335.

30. Block, *Ludus Coventriae,* p. 30.

31. Ibid., p. 32.

32. Tertullian, *Adversus Marcionem, PL,* 2.310:

> Diximus de sacrificiorum rationali institutione, avocantis scilicet ab idolis ad Deum officia ea, quae si rursus ejecerat, dicens: "Quo mihi multitudinem sacrificiorum vestrum?" hoc ipsum voluit intelligi, quod non sibi ea proprie exegisset: "Non enim bibam," inquit, "sanguinem taurorum"; quia et alibi ait: "Deus aeternus non esuriet, nec sitiet." Nam etsi ad oblationes Abel advertit, et holocausta Noe odoratus est libenter, quae jucunditas sive viscerum vervecinorum, sive nidoris ardentium victimarum? Sed animus simplex et Deum metuens offerentium ea quae a Deo habebant, et pabuli et suavis olentiae gratia apud Deum deputabatur, non quae fiebant, exigentis, sed illud propter quod fiebant, ob honorem scilicet Dei.

III • *Processus Noe*

1. Kolve, *Corpus Christi*, p. 106.
2. Josiah Forshall and Frederick Maddens, eds., *The Holy Bible Made from the Latin Vulgate by John Wycliffe and His Followers*, 2:744.
3. Remigius of Auxerre, *Enarrationes in Psalmos*, PL, 131.185. "Quid est homo? quod magnum et quod dignum apud te? video enim fragilem, nullius pretii, et indignum tua dignatione, sed sua culpa, non natura: quia tu creasti eum ad imaginem et similitudinem tuam. . . . Per inobedientiam recesserat a te, et venerat in regionem longinquam: sed tu per misericordiam tuam memor quod ratione tibi similis creatus esset, eum evocasti per filii tui obedientiam."
4. Chambers, *English Literature*, p. 37.
5. Alan Nelson, " 'Sacred' and 'Secular' Currents in the Towneley Play of Noah," p. 396.
6. Ibid.
7. Kolve, *Corpus Christi*, p. 147.
8. Gardner, "Imagery and Illusion," pp. 3–12.
9. Rabanus Maurus, *Commentariorum in Genesim*, PL, 107.513. "Nunquid in Deum poenitentia aut dolor cordis cadere potest? Ira Dei non perturbatio animi ejus est, sed judicium quo irrogatur poena peccato, cogitatio vero ejus et recogitatio mutandarum rerum est immutabilis ratio. Non Deus de facto suo poenitet aut dolet sicut homo, cui est de omnibus rebus omnino tam fixa sententia quam certa praescientia, sed utitur Scriptura sancta usitatis nobis verbis intelligentibus, ut coaptet se nostrae parvitati, quatenus ex cognotis incognita cognoscamus."
10. Gardner, "Imagery and Illusion," p. 4.
11. Rupert of Deutz, *De sancta trinitate et operibus ejus*, PL, 167.341. "Primo sciendum triforme unius Trinitatis esse judicium. Primum videlicet, quo diabolus de coelo dejectus; et ultimum quo idem in fine saeculi cum angelis suis, et malis hominibus in ignem aeternum est mittendus: medium hoc, quo diluvium mundo inducitur."
12. Gardner, "Imagery and Illusion," p. 5.
13. Reginald Pecock, *The Reule of the Crysten Religioun*, p. 72.

14. Thomas Aquinas, *Summa theologiae*, 1:208b.
15. Richard Morris, ed., *Cursor mundi*, 1:41, Trinity MS. In each reference to this text, I have cited the manuscript that is clearest.
16. Gustaf Holmstedt, ed., *Speculum Christiani*, p. 151.

> In þe world what ellis se we
> but wrechidnesse and vanite
> A place it is of grete gylerie
> Of tresun, discorde & tyrauntrie . . .
> Of pryde, of enuy and foule lechery,
> Of sleuth, of wreth and myche glotony,
> Of false couetyse and wynnynge synfully.

17. Kolve, *Corpus Christi*, p. 89.
18. Isidore, *Etymologiarum, PL*, 82.397.

Nam proprie homo ab humo, Graeci autem hominem ἄνθρωπον appellaverunt, eo quod sursum spectet, sublevatus ab humo ad contemplationem artificis sui. Quod Ovidius poeta designat, cum dicit:

> Pronaque cum spectent animalia caetera terram,
> Os homini sublime dedit, coelumque videre
> Jussit, et erectos ad sidera tollere vultus.

Qui ideo erectus coelum aspicit, ut Deum quaerat, non ut terram intendat, veluti pecora, quae natura prona et ventri obedientia finxit."

19. Cawley, *The Wakefield Pageants*, p. xxvi.
20. Rabanus Maurus, *PL*, 107.513. "Si nullus sine peccato, quomodo aliquis perfectus esse potest? Perfecti hic aliqui dicuntur, non sicut perficiendi sunt sancti in illa immortalitate, qua aequabuntur angelis Dei, sed sicut esse possunt in hac peregrinatione perfecti. Unde signanter ait, in generatione sua, ut ostenderet non juxta justitiam consummatam, sed juxta generationis suae eum justum fuisse justitiam."
21. Morris, *Cursor mundi*, 1:61, Trinity MS.
22. Chaucer, The Wife of Bath's Prologue, ll. 154–55, 161–62.
23. Chambers, *English Literature*, p. 37.
24. Block, *Ludus Coventriae*, p. 35.

25. Anna Jean Mill, "Noah's Wife Again," p. 613.

26. The playwright is following a patristic tradition in his domestic parallel to divine wrath. The flood was seen as a beating administered to instill obedience in man, although the following example gives the flogging of a son by his father, rather than of a wife by her husband: " 'Percute,' inquit Scriptura, 'filium tuum virga, et liberabis animam ejus a morte.' Recte igitur et utiliter ut sapientiam Dei decuit, petulantem atque in carne et sanguine lascivientem mundum recentem, tanquam stultum puerulum corripuit, tali percutiens verbere quod tota sua aetate non queat oblivisci." Rupert of Deutz, *De sancta trinitate, PL,* 167.341.

27. To tighten the parallelism between these two creations, the playwright alters the biblical timetable that called for Noah to spend some hundred years in building the ark. The *Glossa ordinaria* repeats Augustine's wonder about the possibility of constructing so great a craft in so short a time: "Quaeritur utrum tam magna arca centum annis potuit fabricari a quator hominibus, id est, Noe et filiis ejus tribus?" Walafrid Strabo, *PL,* 113.107.

28. For a study of the orgins of this tradition see Francis Lee Utley, *The Crooked Rib,* pp. 3–38.

29. Kolve, *Corpus Christi,* p. 254.

30. Deimling, *The Chester Plays,* 1:52.

31. Robert Stevick, *One Hundred Middle English Lyrics,* p. 100.

32. Mill, "Noah's Wife Again," p. 613.

33. Hugh of Saint Victor, *De bestiis et aliis rebus, PL,* 177.31. "Scriptura dicit: 'corvus ad arcam non rediit,' quia forsitan aquis diluvii interceptus periit vel cadaveribus inventis forsitan supersedit, similiter peccator, qui carnalibus desideriis pascitur, quasi corvus qui ad arcam non rediit, curis exterioribus detinetur."

34. Augustine, *Sermones de sanctis, PL,* 39.2028. "Nam et nos, etsi peccatores, ad imitationem Sancti Noe annuntiamus vobis mundi futurum esse excidium; et illos tantummodo dicimus periculum evasuros, quos triplex arca intra se gremio incluserit. Triplex enim arca est Ecclesia, quia Trinitatis continet sacramentum. . . . Annuntiamus igitur sicut Noe, mundi futurum esse naufragium, et ad hanc domum omnes homines admonemus."

35. William Langland, *The Vision of William concerning Piers the Plowman*, 1:321.

36. Kolve, *Corpus Christi*, p. 102.

37. Carleton Brown, ed., *English Lyrics of the Thirteenth Century*, p. 42.

38. Noah is conscious of the difference between himself as workman and the Craftsman who created the world from nothing. The *Cursor mundi*, 1:27, notes this distinction:

> þis wriʒte þat I speke of here
> Is prince ouer alle wiþouten pere
> For oþere wriʒtes mot tymber take
> But he hym self con tymber make.

39. Lucy T. Smith, ed., *York Plays*, p. 43.

40. Carey, *The Wakefield Group*, p. 68, suggests a French source for the idea of God as ruler of the world and pilot of a ship through the ambiguity of the word, "*gubernateur.*"

41. Don Cameron Allen, *The Legend of Noah*, p. 71.

42. Ambrose, *De Noe et arca*, *PL*, 14.407. "Moventur plerique qua causa non dixerit Scriptor, quod etiam uxoris et filiorum Noe memor fuit Dominus. . . . Sed cum dixerit quod Noe memor fuerit, in auctore et praesule domus necessitudines ejus reliqua comprehendit. . . . Etenim cum omnes invicem sibi chari sunt, una est domus; cum autem discrepant, separantur et scinditur in plures domos. Ubi ergo charitas, ibi senioris nomine de quo pendent caeteri, domus omnis significatur."

43. Erich Auerbach, *Mimesis*, p. 52.

IV • *Prima pastorum*

1. Richard Rolle, *The Pricke of Conscience*, p. 40.

2. Ibid., p. 27.

3. Carleton Brown, *Religious Lyrics of the Fourteenth Century*, p. 160.

4. Stanley J. Kahrl, ed., *Merie Tales of the Mad Men of Gotam*, p. x, notes that several of the tales in this collection date back to the twelfth century.

5. W. Carew Hazlitt, ed., "A Hundred Mery Talys," in *Shakespeare Jest Books*, p. 42.

6. As in *Troilus and Criseyde* (Bk. 4, ll. 621–22): "Lat nat this wrecched wo thyn herte gnawe, / But manly sette the world on sexe and seven." In *Magnus Herodes* (Cawley, *The Wakefield Pageants*, p. 67), our playwright also uses this alternate expression: "I shall, and that in hy, set all on sex and seuen."

7. Cf. *Secunda pastorum* (Cawley, *The Wakefield Pageants*, p. 62): "The fader of heuen, God omnypotent, / That sett al on seuen, his son has he sent."

8. Forshall and Maddens, eds., *The Holy Bible*.

9. The shepherd in the Chester version spends twenty-two lines describing possible cures for the rot.

10. Cawley, *The Wakefield Pageants*, p. 113.

11. In Charlotte D'Evelyn and Anna J. Mill, eds., *The South English Legendary*, 1:68, Adam tells his son the following tale:

Euerich stude þat we on stepte • forbarnde vnder
    oure vet
Ne miȝte þer neuer eft gras on growe • & al þe oþer
    wei is grene
For þe voule sunne þat we dude • oure stappes beoþ
    euere sene.

An angel then tells of the time when this stain will be removed:

þe child he sede þat þou iseie • anouwarde þe treo
Godes sone it was þat wol an eorþe • for þi uader
    sunne beo.
And þe oil of milce wiþ him bringe • wanne þetime in
    eld is
And smurie þer wiþ & bringe of pine • þi uader & al
    his.

12. Gordon Gerould, "Moll of the *Prima pastorum*," p. 225.

13. Hazlitt, *Jest Books*, p. 93.

14. Ibid., p. 94.

15. Ibid.

16. England, ed., *The Towneley Plays*, p. 201.

17. W. Nelson Francis, ed., *The Book of Vices and Virtues*, p. 273. Communion is, of course, implied in this feast.

18. Cawley, *The Wakefield Pageants,* p. 22.

19. A. C. Cawley, "The 'Grotesque' Feast in *Prima pastorum,*" p. 215.

20. Francis, *Vices and Virtues,* p. 274.

21. Margery Morgan, " 'High Fraud': Paradox and Double Plot in the English Shepherds' Plays," p. 678.

22. Cawley, "The 'Grotesque' Feast," p. 215.

23. Richard L. Greene, ed., *The Early English Carols,* p. 353.

24. Greene, *Carols,* p. 4.

25. Greene, *Carols,* p. 378, notes the similarity.

26. Francis, *Vices and Virtues,* p. 272.

27. John Lydgate, *The Minor Poems,* 1:103, says this succinctly in discussing the virtues of communion: "Graunt me, Iesu, for a restoratyf, / Thee to receue or I henes pace."

28. Ibid., p. 113.

29. Rolle, *Pricke of Conscience,* pp. 238, 239.

30. Francis A. Foster, ed., *A Stanzaic Life of Christ,* p. 24.

31. Robert Weimann, "Realismus und Simultankonvention im Misteriendrama: Mimesis, Parodie und Utopie in den Towneley-hirtenszene," p. 130.

32. The shepherds have imaginatively skirted the class of gluttony by turning the food into a royal feast: "þe ferþe braunch of Gluttony is in hem þat to nobley and to dentuously wole lyue, þat spendeþ and wasteþ here þrotes to fille hem, wherwiþ many pore men myȝt be sufficiauntly fed" (Francis, *Vices and Virtues,* p. 52).

33. Langland, *Piers the Plowman,* 1:23.

34. Lydgate, *Minor Poems,* p. 107.

35. Eugene B. Cantelupe and Richard Griffeth, "The Gifts of the Shepherds in the Wakefield *Secunda pastorum:* An Iconographical Interpretation," pp. 328–35.

36. Roman Dyboski, ed., *Songs, Carols and Other Miscellaneous Poems,* p. 29.

37. Cantelupe and Griffeth, "Gifts of the Shepherds," p. 330.

38. *Oxford English Dictionary,* s.v. "coffer."

39. Cantelupe and Griffeth, "Gifts of the Shepherds," p. 330.

40. Foster, *Life of Christ,* p. 70.

41. Francis, *Vices and Virtues,* p. 279.

42. Carleton Brown, *Religious Lyrics of the Fifteenth Century,* p. 109.

43. The incense was usually connected with the sacrifice of priesthood, but when sacrifice is attributed to myrrh, incense signifies an unspecified aspect of priesthood.

v • Satan as Everyshepherd

1. A. P. Rossiter, *English Drama from Early Times to the Elizabethans,* p. 72.

2. Thompson, "Unity in *The Second Shepherds' Tale,*" pp. 302–4.

3. Manley, "Shepherds and Prophets," p. 155.

4. Eugene Zumwalt, "Irony of the Towneley Shepherds' Plays," p. 40.

5. Ibid., p. 53.

6. John Speirs, "The Towneley Shepherds' Plays," in *A Guide to English Literature,* 1:161.

7. Prosser, *Drama and Religion,* p. 61.

8. Speirs, "The Towneley Shepherds' Plays," p. 159.

9. Zumwalt, "Irony," p. 43.

10. Hardin Craig, ed., *Two Coventry Corpus Christi Plays,* p. 7.

11. Manley, "Shepherds and Prophets," p. 153.

12. Craig, *Two Coventry Corpus Christi Plays,* p. 10.

13. Brown, *Religious Lyrics of the Fourteenth Century,* p. 10.

14. There is another possible image of life as an abortive endeavor, although this would move the first known instance of *miscarry* in this sense back by a hundred years: "Thus ar husbandys oprest, in ponte to myscary / on lyfe" (22–23).

15. Cawley, *The Wakefield Pageants,* p. 105.

16. Zumwalt, "Irony," p. 49, says, "The . . . poet has developed this pejorative theme about marriage, maternity and childing and put it inextricably at the heart of his greatest drama."

17. "The Thrush and the Nightingale," in Brown, *English Lyrics of the Thirteenth Century*, p. 101, provides an example of this structure in the *débat*.

18. Brown, *English Lyrics of the Thirteenth Century*, p. 141.

19. Ibid.

20. Ibid., p. 142.

21. Nan Cooke Carpenter, "Music in the *Secunda pastorum*," in *Medieval English Drama*, ed. Jerome Taylor and Alan Nelson, p. 213.

22. Thomas Simmons and Henry Nolloth, eds., *Lay Folks Catechism*, p. 78: "For nouthir sal we fall so ferr in al wanhope / That we ne sall traist to have blisse if we wele do."

24. Craig, *Two Coventry Corpus Christi Plays*, p. 8.

25. Kemp Malone, "A Note on the Towneley *Secunda pastorum*," p. 38.

26. Claude Chidamian, "Mak and the Tossing in the Blanket," p. 186.

27. Ibid., p. 187.

28. Ibid., p. 189. Italics mine.

29. Hans Kurath, ed., *Middle English Dictionary*, s.v. "abort."

30. Carpenter, "Music in the *Secunda pastorum*," p. 214.

31. This seems to be an inversion of the sophisticated devil from the north country who is presented, for example, in Chaucer's Friar's Tale.

32. England, *The Towneley Plays*, p. 3.

33. Augustine, *Sermones de Scripturis*, PL, 38.532. "Erimus ergo in illa mercede omnes aequales . . . quia denarius ille vita aeterna est, et in vita aeterna omnes aequales erunt." Cawley, *The Wakefield Pageants*, p. 109, points out this reference to the parable.

34. Manley, "Shepherds and Prophets," p. 155.

35. Stith Thompson, *Motif Index of Folk-literature*, 4:256 (K 218.1); 2:207 (D 1381.11).

36. Francis Thompson, "Unity," p. 304.

37. See, for example, the Pardoner's lie and the Palmer's answer in *The Playe Called the Foure PP*, in *Chief Pre-Shakespearean Dramas*, ed. Joseph Q. Adams, p. 380.

38. Rabanus Maurus, *De Universo, PL,* 111.223: "Lupus . . . raro invenitur bonam significationem habere sed saepius contrarium. Nam aut diabolum significat, ut est illud in Evangelio: 'videt lupum venientem, et dimittit oves, et fugit.' "

39. Florence McCulloch, *Medieval Latin and French Bestiaries,* p. 189.

40. Rabanus Maurus, *PL,* 111.223, "rapax bestia et cruoris appetens."

41. Ibid., "famem diu portant."

42. Ibid., "et post longa ieiunia multum devorant."

43. Chambers, *English Literature,* p. 38.

44. Homer Watt, "The Dramatic Unity of the *Secunda pastorum,*" in *Essays and Studies in Honor of Carleton Brown,* p. 161.

45. Greene, *The Early English Carols,* p. 106. There are five more stanzas to the same effect.

46. On the gifts see John P. Cutts, "The Shepherds' Gifts in *The Second Shepherds' Play* and Bosch's 'Adoration of the Magi,' " pp. 120–24; Cantelupe and Griffeth, "The Gifts of the Shepherds," pp. 328–35; and Lawrence J. Ross, "Symbol and Structure in the *Secunda pastorum,*" pp. 177–211.

47. Cawley, *The Wakefield Pageants,* p. 113.

VI • Herod as Antichrist

1. Meyers, *A Figure Given,* passim.

2. Isidore, *Allegoriae quaedam sacrae scripturae, PL,* 83.118. "Herodes, qui infantibus necem intulit, diaboli formam expressit, vel gentium qui, cupientes extinguere nomen Christi de mundo, in caede martyrum saevierunt."

3. Adam the Scot, *Sermones in epiphania Domini, PL,* 198.398. "Utramque enim interpretationem in se habet Herodes. Beemoth loquor quem in Evangelio Dominus fortem armatum appellat 'cujus fortitudo in lumbis ejus et virtus illius in umbilico ventris ejus, omne sublime videns, rex est super omnes filios superbiae.' Imperat hodie super terram, et suam potenter tyrannidem exercet, princeps illi mundi, serpens antiquus, qui vocatur diabolus et Satanas."

4. Morris, *Cursor mundi,* 4:1264, Cotton MS.

5. Meyers, *A Figure Given,* p. 53, notes this is common among the types of Satan in the Wakefield plays.

6. Rupert of Deutz, *De victoria verbi Dei, PL,* 169.1174. "Primus namque draconis hujus hiatus fuit, ubi secundum Matthaeum mox nati pueri animam, sicut superius dictum est, funestus Herodes quaesivit, et propter eum infantes occidit."

7. Karl Young, *Drama of the Medieval Church,* 2:497. "Ergo de Antichristo scire volentes primo notabitis quare sic vocatus sit. Ideo scilicet, quia Christo in cunctis contrarius erit, id est Christo contraria faciet. Christus venit humilis, ille venturus est superbus. Christus venit humiles erigere, peccatores iustificare; ille e contra humiles deiciet, peccatores magnificabit, impios exaltabit semperque vitia quae sunt contraria virtutibus docebit."

8. Morris, *Cursor mundi,* 4:1266, Fairfax MS.

9. England, *The Towneley Plays,* p. 195:

> I am send bot messyngere
> ffrom hym that alkyn mys may mend;
> I go before, bodword to bere,
> And as forgangere am I send,
> his wayes to wyse, his lawes to lere,
> Both man and wyfe that has offende.
> ffull mekyll barett mon he bere,
> Or tyme he haue broght all tyll ende.

10. Morris, *Cursor mundi,* 4:1266, Fairfax MS.

11. Heresis and Ypocrisis, the henchmen of Antichrist in the Tegernsee *Ludus de Antichristo,* remind their master: "Per nos mundus tibi credet; / Nomen Christi tibi cedet." Young, *Drama of the Medieval Church,* 2:378.

12. Cawley, *The Wakefield Pageants,* p. 114.

13. In the *Prima pastorum,* for example, the first shepherd greets the infant Christ with the same words: "Hayll, the worthyest of all! Hayll duke! Hayll, knyght!" Cawley, *The Wakefield Pageants,* p. 41.

14. Meyers, *A Figure Given,* p. 71.

15. Morris, *Cursor mundi,* 4:1266, Fairfax MS.

16. Ibid.

17. Meyers, *A Figure Given*, p. 73.

18. Arnoul Greban, *Le Mystère de la Passion*, p. 80.

> Fortune, il n'en pas in toy,
> Fortune, beste merveillable:
> toy et ta roue detestable
> mettons au sanglant pis tourner.

19. Gregory the Great, *Moralia in Job, PL*, 75.1053. "Memoriam vero suam in terra statuere Antichristus conatur, cum in terrena gloria appetit esset possibile, in perpetuum permanere. Nomen suum in plateis celebrari gaudet, cum longe lateque operationem suae iniquitatis extendit. Sed quia diu haec ejus iniquitas non sinitur extolli, dicatur: Memoria illius pereat de terra, et non celebratur nomen ejus in plateis."

20. Edward K. Rand, *Founders of the Middle Ages*, p. 12, translates this passage.

21. Morris, *Cursor mundi*, 4:1258, Fairfax MS.

22. Cawley, *The Wakefield Pageants*, p. 116.

23. Morris, *Cursor mundi*, 4:1258, Fairfax MS.

24. Gregory, *Moralia, PL*, 75.484. "Jam in membris suis vivit et saevit Antichristus. . . . Cain tempus Antichristi non vidit, et tamen membrum Antichristi per meritum fuit."

25. Young, *Drama of the Medieval Church*, 2:380. "Vive per gratiam et suscipe honorem dum recognoscis cunctorum creatorem."

26. Cawley, *The Wakefield Pageants*, p. 41.

27. John M. Manly, ed., *Specimens of the Pre-Shakespearean Drama*, 1:179.

28. In terms of the parody mass described below, this payoff would correspond to the popular notion that the mass penny was a cash investment:

> And þi peny him profre,
> þauȝ þou be not þer-to in dette,
> þou schalt þinke hit ful wel bi-set, . . .
> of sinnes hit wol make þe to sese,
> And þi catel also encrese
> Of Seluer in þi Cofre.

Thomas Simmons, ed., *The Lay Folks Mass Book*, p. 142.

29. Lydgate, *Minor poems*, 1:93.
30. J. Matthews, ed., *The Chester Plays*, 2:388.
31. Morris, *Cursor mundi*, 4:1268, Fairfax MS.
32. Matthews, *The Chester Plays*, 2:389.
33. Deimling, *The Chester Plays*, 1:201.
34. Greban, *Mystère de la Passion*, p. 102:

> je vis et la mort m'est devant
> je meurs et je suis tout vivant
> j'enrage et je suis tout sensible,
> et cuide qu'il n'est point possible
> qu'onque homme fust ainsi pugny.

35. Paul the Deacon, *Homiliae de tempore*, *PL*, 85.1174. "Herodes stridet cadens ipse in laqueum quem tetendit, hinc iniquitatem quam considerat, evaginat."
36. Gregory, *Moralia*, *PL*, 75.652. "Daniel et Paulus de Antichristo eadem docent: . . . contra principem principum consurget, et sine manu conteretur. Sine manu quippe conteretur, quia non angelorum bello, non sanctorum certamine, sed per adventum judicis solo oris spiritu aeterna morte ferietur."
37. Greban, *Mystère de la Passion*, p. 102:

> haro! quelz tourmens importables:
> ie vois plus de cent mille deables,
> le plus hideux qu'on scent comprendre,
> qui n'attendent que pour moy prendre
> et moy entrainer avec eulx.

38. Matthews, *The Chester Plays*, 2:410.
39. Gregory, *Moralia*, *PL*, 75.717. "Diabolus tanto acrius saevit, quanto poenae consummationi est vicinior."
40. Matthews, *The Chester Plays*, 2:413.
41. Young, *Drama of the Medieval Church*, 2:105. "Quare non defendis sanguinem nostrum? . . . Adhuc sustinete modicum tempus, donec impleatur numerus fratrum uestrorum."
42. Ibid. "Tu, que tristaris, exulta, que lacrimaris, / Namque tui nati uiuunt super astra beati."
43. Gregory, *Moralia*, *PL*, 75.717. "Considerat quippe quod juxta sit ut licentiam nequissimae libertatis amittat, et

quantum brevitate temporis angustatur, tantum multiplici-
tate crudelitatis expanditur, sicut de illo voce angelica ad
Joannem dicitur: vae terrae et mari, quia descendit diabolus
ad vos habens iram magnam, sciens quod modicum tempus
habet."

44. England, *The Towneley Plays*, p. 362.

45. Louis Duchesne, *Christian Worship: Its Origin and
Evolution*, p. 178. "Quotiescumque hoc feceritis, toties
commemorationem mei facietis, donec iterum adveniam."

46. Lydgate, *Minor Poems*, 1:88.

47. Simmons, *Lay Folks Mass Book*, p. 42.

48. Lydgate, *Minor Poems*, 1:88.

49. John Blunt, ed., *The Myroure of Oure Ladye*, p. 83.
"Ye begynne the *Inuitatory*. that ys as moche to say. as a
callynge. or a sturrynge. Wherby eche of you sturreth. and
exhorteth other to the praysyng of god. & of oure lady. And
therby also. ye calle them that here you: and desyre other
that ar absente to come to prayse with you."

50. William Maskell, *The Ancient Liturgy of the Church
of England*, p. 98. "Orate fratres et sorores pro me pecca-
tore: ut meum pariter vestrum Domino Deo acceptum sit
sacrificium."

51. Lydgate, in the "Meritae Missae" (Simmons, *Lay
Folks Mass Book*, app. 6, p. 153), notes that those who
push to obtain precedence at Mass are the first to run away
in battle:

> In Envye they may be allsoo,
> That no man schould be-for hem goo.
> Be svyche men, I onder-stonde,
> May be the sawacyon of all a londe!
> Schameles and brethelis—(that nowt thee
> May do) all a contre fle.

Similar behavior would be expected of the murderers of
children and conquerors of women that we find in the
Herod play.

52. As in "why Adam ne hiled nouȝt first he mouth þat
eet þe apple Rather þan his lykam *alow*." Kurath, *Middle
English Dictionary*, s.v. "aloue."

53. This prayer, which opens the Canon of the Mass,
"Te igitur Clementissime Pater, per Iesum Christum Filium

tuum Dominum nostrum supplices rogamus ac petimus: Uti accepta habeas et benedicas haec dona, haec munera, haec Sancta sacrificia illibata," might be seen by Herod's minions as a petition for payment for their work of sacrificing the Innocents (Simmons, *Lay Folks Mass Book,* p. 104).

54. Lydgate, *Minor Poems,* 1:97.

55. Gregory the Great, *Liber sacramentorum, PL,* 78.25. "Postmodum legitur Evangelium, deinde offertorium, et dicitur oratio super oblata."

56. Maskell, *Ancient Liturgy,* p. 10.

57. Ibid., p. 130, italics mine. "Hanc igitur oblationem servitutis nostrae, sed et cunctae familiae tuae, quaesumus, Domine, ut placatus accipias: diesque nostros in tua pace disponas, atque ab aeterna damnatione nos eripi, et in electorum tuorum jubeas grege numerari."

58. The triple breast beating during the confession of the Roman use does not exist in the English liturgy, but breast beating is called for in all the English uses except York at the prayer, "Nobis quoque peccatoribus famulis tuis" (Simmons, *Lay Folks Mass Book,* p. 254).

59. Maskell, *Ancient Liturgy,* p. 115.

60. Simmons, *Lay Folks Mass Book,* p. 38.

61. Ibid., p. 285.

62. "I was castyn in care so frightly afrayd; / Bot I that not dyspare, for low is he layd" (478–79).

63. In *The Scourging* of this cycle, Pilate tries to wash the blood from his hands:

> Now that I am sakles of this bloode shall ye see;
> Both my handys in expres weshen sall be;
> This bloode bees dere boght I ges that ye spill so frele.

England, *The Towneley Plays,* p. 250.

64. Simmons, *Lay Folks Mass Book,* p. 143. There is a second ablution in this service after the Communion (p. 145).

65. Blunt, *Myroure of Oure Ladye,* p. 314.

66. Paul the Deacon, *PL,* 95.1175. "Christus futurorum praescius, conscius secretorum, cogitationum judex, mentium perscrutator, quare deseruit quos sciebat quaerendos esse propter se, et propter se noverat occidendos?"

67. Ibid. "Fratres, Cristus non despexit suos milites, sed provexit, quibus ante dedit triumphare quam vivere, quos fecit capere sine concertatione victoriam, quos donavit coronis antequam membris, quos voluit virtutibus vitia praeterire, ante coelum possidere quam terram."

VII • *Coliphizacio*

1. Brown, *Religious Lyrics of the Fifteenth Century*, p. 171.
2. Ibid.
3. Rabanus Maurus, *Commentaria in Matthaeum, PL,* 107.1122. "Alii autem palmas in faciem ei dederunt, dicentes: Prophetiza nobis, Christe, quis est qui percussit? Qui tunc caesus est colaphis sive alapis Judaeorum, caeditur etiam nunc blasphemis falsorum Christianorum.
4. Anderson, *Drama and Imagery*, p. 26.
5. Emile Mâle, *The Gothic Image*, p. 170.
6. Richard Rolle, *English Writings*, p. 20.
7. Hilary of Poitiers, *Commentarius in Evangelium Matthaei, PL,* 9.1074. "In palmis vero atque sputis, ad consummandam hominis humilitatem universa in eum contumelarium genera exercebantur."
8. Brown, *Religious Lyrics of the Fourteenth Century,* p. 16.
9. England, *The Towneley Plays*, p. 226.
10. Block, *Ludus Coventriae*, p. 275.
11. Paul Vignaux, *Philosophy in the Middle Ages*, p. 53. "Est autem vox, Boethio texte, aeris per linguam percussio."
12. Ibid. "Significare autem vel monstrare vocum est."
13. Peter Abelard, *Dialectica*, p. 127. "Hircocervus significat aliquid . . . nomen est rei non-existentis."
14. In the Lazarus play, Mary connects the stone with the corruption of death (England, *The Towneley Plays*, p. 389):

> lorde, if it be thi Will,
> I hope be this he savers ill,

ffor it is now the ferth day gone
sen he Was laid vnder yone stone.

15. Langland, *Piers the Plowman,* 1:15. In addition to this example, *London Licpenye* (Eleanor P. Hammond, ed., *English Verse between Chaucer and Surrey,* p. 238) records the adventures of a poverty-stricken young man who tries in vain to get legal aid without money:

I tolde hym my case, as well as I coude
and seynd all my goods by nowrd and by sowde
I am defrawdyd with great falshed
he would not geve me a momme of his mouthe
for lake of money I may not spede.

16. England, *The Towneley Plays,* p. 367.

17. Paschasius Radbertus, *Expositio in Mattheum, PL,* 120.923. "Quia quanto benignissimus Jesus plus tacebat intrepidus magis ille [Caiaphas] amentia superatus, eum ad respondendum provocat qualibet occasione sermonis, si forte locum inveniat accusandi."

18. The Old Testament is always on the left side in pictures showing the two testaments.

19. Paschasius Radbertus, *Expositio, PL,* 120.923. "Jesus autem tacebat, indignum eum sua responsione decernens juxta illud propheticum: 'Dum consisteret adversum me peccator, obmutui, et humiliatus sum nimis et silui a bonis.' "

20. Abelard, *Dialectica,* p. 576. "Neque enim vox aliqua naturaliter rei significatae inest, sed secundum hominum impositionem."

21. Ella K. Whiting, ed., *The Poems of John Audelay,* p. 67:

ȝif þou to þe cherche go
To-ward, fro-ward, or ellis cum from,
To here masse ȝif þou may,
Al þe way þat þou gase
An angel payntus þi face
þe Prynce of heuen to pay.

22. England, *The Towneley Plays,* p. 310.

23. Rabanus Maurus, *Commentaria, PL,* 107.1122:

Velaverunt autem faciem ejus, secundum quod Marcus Judaeos tunc fecisse commemorat, non ut eorum scelera non videat, sed ut a se ipsis, sicut quondam Moysi ferunt, gratiam cognitionis ejus abscondant. Si enim crederent Moysi, crederent forsitan et Domino. Quod velamentum usque hodie manet super cor eorum non revelatum, nobis autem in Christum credentibus ablatum est. Neque enim frustra eo moriente velum templi scissum est medium, et ea quae toto legis tempore latuerant, et abscondita carnali Israel fuerant, Novi Testamenti cultoribus sunt patefacta sancta sanctorum arcana.

24. Barry Sanders, "Who's Afraid of Jesus Christ? Games in the *Coliphizacio*," p. 97.
25. Erwin Panofsky, *Studies in Iconology*, p. 109.
26. England, *The Towneley Plays*, p. 251.

> This cros vp thou take
> and make the redy bowne;
> Withoutt gruchyng thou rake
> and bere it thrugh the towne.

27. Ibid., p. 274.
28. Ibid., p. 262.
29. Smith, *York Plays*, p. 362.

> To saue nowe þi selffe late vs see,
> God sonne if þou grthely be grayde,
> Delyuere þe doune of þat tree.

30. Block, *Ludus Coventriae*, p. 276.
31. England, *The Towneley Plays*, p. 367.

VIII • Symbolic Action

1. O. B. Hardison, *Christian Rite and Christian Drama in the Middle Ages*, p. 11.
2. Ibid., p. 16.
3. Charles De Tolnay, *Hieronymus Bosch*, p. 350.
4. Ibid., p. 290.

5. Gustav Glück, *Bruegels Gemälde*, p. 45, my translation.

6. Jacques Lassaigne and Robert Delevoy, *Flemish Painting*, p. 50.

7. Glück, *Bruegels Gemälde*, p. 56.

8. Kolve, *Corpus Christi*, p. 101.

9. Glynne Wickham, *Early English Stages*, 1:173.

10. Richard Southern, *The Medieval Theatre in the Round*.

11. Stanley J. Kahrl, *Traditions of Medieval English Drama*, p. 46.

12. Kolve, *Corpus Christi*, pp. 101–23.

Bibliography

Medieval Texts

Abelard, Peter. *Dialectica.* Edited by L. M. De Reijk. Assen, Netherlands: Koninklijke Van Gorcum & Co., 1956.

Adam the Scot. *Sermones in epiphania Domini. Patrologia Latina,* 198.393–410. Paris: J.-P. Migne, 1855.

Adams, Joseph Q., ed. *Chief Pre-Shakespearean Dramas.* Cambridge, Mass.: Houghton Mifflin, 1924.

Ambrose. *De Cain et Abel. Patrologia Latina,* 14.315–60. Paris: J.-P. Migne, 1845.

————. *De Noe et arca. Patrologia Latina,* 14.361–416. Paris: J.-P. Migne, 1845.

————. *De poenitentia. Patrologia Latina,* 17.969–1004. Paris: J.-P. Migne, 1845.

Aquinas, Thomas. *Summa theologiae.* Vol 1. Ottawa: Institute of Medieval Studies, 1941.

Augustine. *De civitate Dei. Patrologia Latina,* Vol. 41. Paris: J.-P. Migne, 1841.

————. *Les Confessions.* Bibliothèque Augustinienne, 2d series, 13. Paris: Desclée de Brouwer, 1962.

————. *Sermones de sanctis. Patrologia Latina,* 39.2095–2172. Paris: J.-P. Migne, 1845.

————. *Sermones de scripturis. Patrologia Latina,* 38.23–994. Paris: J.-P. Migne, 1841.

————. *La Trinité.* Bibliothèque Augustinienne, 2d series, 16. Paris: Desclée de Brouwer, 1955.

Banks, Mary Macleod, ed. *An Alphabet of Tales.* Vol. 1. Early English Text Society. o.s., no. 126. London: N. Trübner & Co., 1904.

Block, K. S., ed. *Ludus Coventriae.* Early English Text Society, e.s., no. 120. Oxford: Oxford University Press, 1922.

Blunt, John, ed. *The Myroure of Oure Ladye.* Early English Text Society, e.s., no. 19. London: N. Trübner, 1873.

Brown, Carleton, ed. *English Lyrics of the Thirteenth Century.* Oxford: Clarendon Press, 1932.

————, ed. *Religious Lyrics of the Fifteenth Century.* Oxford: Clarendon Press, 1936.

————, ed. *Religious Lyrics of the Fourteenth Century.* Oxford: Clarendon Press, 1924.

Craig, Hardin, ed. *Two Coventry Corpus Christi Plays.* Early English Text Society, e.s., no. 87. London: Oxford University Press, 1952.

Deimling, Hermann, ed. *The Chester Plays.* Vol. 1. Early English Text Society, e.s., no. 62. Oxford: K. Paul, Trench, Trübner & Co., 1892.

D'Evelyn, Charlotte, and Anna J. Mill, eds. *The South English Legendary.* Vol 1. Early English Text Society, o.s., no. 235. London: Oxford University Press, 1951.

Dyboski, Roman, ed. *Songs, Carols and Other Miscellaneous Poems.* Early English Text Society, e.s., no. 101. London: K. Paul, Trench, Trübner & Co., 1907.

England, George, ed. *The Towneley Plays.* Early English Text Society, e.s., no. 71. London: K. Paul, Trench, Trübner & Co., 1897.

Forshall, Josiah, and Frederick Maddens, eds. *The Holy Bible Made from the Latin Vulgate by John Wycliffe and His Followers.* Oxford: University Press, 1850.

Foster, Francis A., ed. *A Stanzaic Life of Christ.* Early English Text Society, o.s., no. 166. London: Oxford University Press, 1904.

Francis, W. Nelson, ed. *The Book of Vices and Virtues.* Early English Text Society, o.s. 217. London: Oxford University Press, 1942.

Greban, Arnoul. *Le Mystère de la Passion.* Edited by Gaston Paris and Gaston Raynaud. Paris: F. Vieweg, 1878.

Greene, Richard L., ed. *The Early English Carols.* Oxford: Clarendon Press, 1935.

Gregory the Great. *Moralia in Job.* Patrologia Latina, 75:510–1162. Paris: J.-P. Migne, 1849.

Hammond, Eleanor P., ed. *English Verse between Chaucer and Surrey.* Durham: Duke University Press, 1927.

Hazlitt, W. Carew, ed. *Shakespeare Jest Books.* London: H. Sotheran & Co., 1881.

Hilary of Poitiers. *Commentarius in Evangelium Matthaei.* Patrologia Latina, 9.917–1078. Paris: J.-P. Migne, 1844.

Holmstedt, Gustaf, ed. *Speculum Christiani.* Early English

Text Society, o.s., no. 182. London: Oxford University Press, 1933.

Hugh of Saint Victor. *Adnotationes elucidatorie in Pentateuchon. Patrologia Latina*, 175.29–86. Paris: J.-P. Migne, 1854.

————. *De bestiis et aliis rebus. Patrologia Latina*, 177.9–164. Paris: J.-P. Migne, 1854.

Isidore. *Allegoriae quaedam sacrae scripturae. Patrologia Latina*, 83.98–130. Paris: J.-P. Migne, 1850.

————. *Etymologiarum. Patrologia Latina*, 82.9–728. Paris: J.-P. Migne, 1850.

Jerome. *Commentarii in Epistolas B. Pauli. Patrologia Latina*, 30.531–902. Paris: J.-P. Migne, 1846.

Kahrl, Stanley J. ed. *Merie Tales of the Mad Men of Gotam.* Evanston, Ill.: Northwestern University Press, 1965.

Langland, William. *The Vision of William concerning Piers the Plowman.* 2 vols. Edited by Walter W. Skeat. Oxford: Clarendon Press, 1886.

Lydgate, John. *The Minor Poems.* Vol. 1. Edited by Henry MacCracken. Early English Text Society, e.s., no. 107. London: K. Paul, Trench, Trübner & Co., 1911.

Manly, John M., ed. *Specimens of the Pre-Shaksperean Drama.* Vol. 1. Boston: Ginn & Co., 1897.

Matthews, J., ed. *The Chester Plays.* Vol. 2. Early English Text Society, e.s., no. 115. London: K. Paul, Trench, Trübner & Co., 1916.

Morris, Richard, ed. *Cursor mundi.* Vols. 1, 4. Early English Text Society, o.s., nos. 57, 66. London: K. Paul, Trench, Trübner & Co., 1874.

Paschasius Radbertus. *Expositio in Matthaeum. Patrologia Latina*, 120.31–994. Paris: J.-P. Migne, 1852.

Paul the Deacon. *Homiliae de tempore. Patrologia Latina*, 95.1159–1582. Paris: J.-P. Migne, 1851.

Pecock, Reginald. *The Reule of the Crysten Religioun.* Early English Text Society, o.s., no. 171. London: Oxford University Press, 1927.

Rabanus Maurus. *Commentaria in Matthaeum. Patrologia Latina*, 107.727–1156. Paris: J.-P. Migne, 1851.

————. *Commentariorum in Genesim. Patrologia Latina*, 117.439–670. Paris: J.-P. Migne, 1851.

————. *De universo. Patrologia Latina,* 111.9–613. Paris: J.-P. Migne, 1852.

Remigius of Auxerre. *Enarrationes in Psalmos. Patrologia Latina,* 131.134–844. Paris: J.-P. Migne, 1853.

Robinson, F. N., ed. *The Works of Geoffrey Chaucer.* 2nd ed. Cambridge, Mass.: Houghton Mifflin, 1957.

Rolle, Richard. *English Writings.* Edited by Hope E. Allen. Oxford: Clarendon Press, 1931.

————. *The Pricke of Conscience.* Edited by Richard Morris. Berlin: Asher & Co., 1863.

Rothschild, James de, ed. *Le Mistère du Viel Testament.* Vol. 1. Paris: Firmin Didot et cie., 1878.

Rupert of Deutz. *De sancta trinitate et operibus ejus. Patrologia Latina,* 167.198–1570. Paris: J.-P. Migne, 1854.

————. *De victoria verbi Dei. Patrologia Latina,* 169.1215–1502. Paris: J.-P. Migne, 1854.

Schmeller, J. A., ed. *Carmina Burana.* Stuttgart: Litterarischer Verein, 1847.

Simmons, Thomas, and Henry Nolloth, eds. *Lay Folks Catechism.* Early English Text Society, o.s., no. 118. London: K. Paul, Trench, Trübner & Co., 1901.

Simmons, Thomas, ed. *The Lay Folks Mass Book.* Early English Text Society, o.s., no. 71. London: N. Trübner & Co., 1879.

Sinclair, John D., trans. *Dante's Inferno.* New York: Galaxy, 1961.

————. *Dante's Purgaturio.* New York: Galaxy, 1961.

Smith, Lucy T. *York Plays.* 1885. Reprint. New York: Russell & Russell, 1963.

Stevick, Robert, ed. *One Hundred Middle English Lyrics.* New York: Bobbs Merrill, 1964.

Tertullian. *Adversus Marcionem. Patrologia Latina,* 2.239–524. Paris: J.-P. Migne, 1844.

Whiting, Ella K., ed. *The Poems of John Audelay.* Early English Text Society, o.s., no. 184. London: Oxford University Press, 1931.

Critical Works

Allen, Don Cameron. *The Legend of Noah.* Urbana: University of Illinois Press, 1949.

Anderson, M. D. *Drama and Imagery in English Medieval Churches*. Cambridge: Cambridge University Press, 1963.

Auerbach, Erich. *Mimesis*. 1953. Reprint. New York: Anchor, 1957.

————. *Scenes from the Drama of European Literature*. New York: Meridien Books, 1959.

Bethurum, Dorothy, ed. *Critical Approaches to Medieval Literature*. New York: Columbia University Press.

Blanch, Robert J. "The Symbolic Gifts of the Shepherds in the *Secunda pastorum*." *Tennessee Studies in Literature* 17 (1972):25–36.

Bloomfield, Morton. "Symbolism in Medieval Literature." *Modern Philology* 56 (1958):73–81.

Campbell, Josie P. "The Idea of Order in the Wakefield *Noah*." *Chaucer Review* 10 (1975):76–86.

Campbell, Thomas. "Why Do the Shepherds Prophesy?" *Comparative Drama* 12 (1978):137–150.

Cantelupe, Eugene B., and Richard Griffeth. "The Gifts of the Shepherds in the Wakefield *Secunda pastorum:* An Iconographical Interpretation." *Medieval Studies* 28 (1966):328–35.

Carey, Millicent. *The Wakefield Group in the Towneley Cycle*. Hesperia, no. 11. Baltimore: Johns Hopkins Press, 1930.

Carpenter, Nan Cooke. "Music in the *Secunda pastorum*." In *Medieval English Drama*, edited by Jerome Taylor and Alan Nelson. Chicago: University of Chicago Press, 1972.

Cawley, A. C. "The 'Grotesque' Feast in *Prima pastorum*." *Speculum* 30 (1955):213–17.

————, ed. *The Wakefield Pageants in the Towneley Cycle*. Manchester: Manchester University Press, 1958.

Chambers, E. K. *English Literature at the Close of the Middle Ages*. Oxford: Clarendon Press, 1945.

Chidamian, Claude. "Mak and the Tossing in the Blanket." *Speculum* 22 (1947):186–90.

Claessens, Bob, and Jeanne Rousseau. *Our Brueghel*. Antwerp: Mercatorfonds, 1969.

Combe, Jacques. *Jerome Bosch*. Paris: Pierre Tisné, 1957.

Cutts, John P. "The Shepherds' Gifts in *The Second Shep-*

herds' Play and Bosch's 'Adoration of the Magi.' " *Comparative Drama* 4 (1970):120–24.

Denny, Neville, ed. *Medieval Drama.* Stratford-upon-Avon Studies, no. 16. London: Edward Arnold, 1973.

De Tolnay, Charles. *Hieronymus Bosch.* London: Methuen, 1966.

Duchesne, Louis. *Christian Worship: Its Origin and Evolution.* London: Macmillan, 1923.

Duncan, Robert L. "Comedy in the English Mysteries." *Illinois Quarterly* 35 (1973):5–14.

Earl, James. "The Shape of Old Testament History in the Towneley Plays." *Studies in Philology* 69 (1972):434–52.

Edwards, Robert. "Techniques of Transcendance in Medieval Drama." *Comparative Drama* 8 (1974):157–71.

Gardner, John. *The Construction of the Wakefield Cycle.* Carbondale: Southern Illinois University Press, 1974.

―――. "Imagery and Illusion in the Wakefield Noah Play." *Papers in Language and Literature* 4 (1968):3–12.

―――. "Theme and Irony in the Wakefield *Mactacio Abel.*" *PMLA* 80 (1965):515–521.

Gayley, Charles. *Plays of Our Forefathers.* New York: Duffield & Co., 1907.

Gerould, Gordon. "Moll of the *Prima pastorum.*" *MLN* 19 (1904):225–30.

Glück, Gustav. *Bruegels Gemälde.* Vienna: A. Schroll, 1932.

Hardison, O. B. *Christian Rite and Christian Drama in the Middle Ages.* Baltimore: Johns Hopkins Press, 1965.

Jambeck, Thomas. "The Canvas-Tossing Allusion in the *Secunda pastorum.*" *Modern Philology* 76 (1978):49–54.

Kahrl, Stanley J. *Traditions of Medieval English Drama.* London: Hutchinson, 1974.

Kolve, V. A. *The Play Called Corpus Christi.* Stanford: Stanford University Press, 1961.

Kurath, Hans, ed. *Middle English Dictionary.* Pt. A. Ann Arbor: University of Michigan Press, 1956.

Lassaigne, Jacques and Robert Delevoy. *Flemish Painting.* New York: Skira, 1958.

Leonard, Frances M. "The School for Transformation: A Theory of Middle English Comedy." *Genre* 9 (1976):179–91.

Linfert, Carl. *Hieronymus Bosch.* New York: Abrams, 1972.

McCulloch, Florence. *Medieval Latin and French Bestiaries.* Studies in the Romance Languages and Literatures, no. 33. Chapel Hill: University of North Carolina Press, 1960.

Mack, Maynard, Jr. "*The Second Shepherds' Play:* A Reconsideration." *PMLA* 93 (1978):78–85.

Mâle, Emile. *The Gothic Image.* New York: Harper Torchbooks, 1968.

Malone, Kemp. "A Note on the Towneley *Secunda pastorum.*" *MLN* 40 (1925):35–39.

Manley, William. "Shepherds and Prophets: Religious Unity in the Towneley *Secunda pastorum.*" *PMLA* 68 (1963):151–55.

Marshall, Linda E. " 'Sacral Parody' in the *Secunda pastorum.*" *Speculum* 47 (1972):720–36.

Maskell, William. *The Ancient Liturgy of the Church of England.* Oxford: Clarendon Press, 1882.

Meyers, Walter E. *A Figure Given: Typology in the Wakefield Plays.* Pittsburgh: Duquesne University Press, 1968.

———. "Typology and the Audience of the English Cycle Plays." *Studies in the Literary Imagination* 8 (1975):145–58.

Mill, Anna Jean. "Noah's Wife Again." *PMLA* 56 (1941):613–26.

Morgan, Margery. " 'High Fraud': Paradox and Double Plot in the English Shepherds' Plays." *Speculum* 39 (1964):676–89.

Munson, William F. "Audience and Meaning in Two Medieval Dramatic Realisms." *Comparative Drama* 9 (1975):44–67.

Nelson, Alan H. *The Medieval English Stage: Corpus Christi Pageants and Plays.* Chicago: University of Chicago Press, 1974.

———. " 'Sacred' and 'Secular' Currents in the Towneley Play of *Noah.*" *Drama Survey* 3 (1964):393–401.

Owst, G. R. *Literature and Pulpit in Medieval England.* 1933. Reprint. Cambridge: Cambridge University Press, 1963.

Panofsky, Erwin. *Studies in Iconology. 1939. Reprint. New York: Harper, 1962.*

Pollack, Rhoda-Gale. "Demonic Imagery in the English Mystery Cycles." *Theatre Notebook* 32 (1978):52–62.

Potter, Robert. *The English Morality Play: Origins, History, and Influence of a Dramatic Tradition.* London: Routledge & Kegan Paul, 1975.

Prosser, Eleanor. *Drama and Religion in the English Mystery Plays.* Stanford Studies in Language and Literature, no. 23. Stanford: Stanford University Press, 1961.

Rand, Edward K. *Founders of the Middle Ages.* 1928. Reprint. New York: Dover, 1957.

Robinson, J. W. "The Art of the York Realist." *Modern Philology* (1962):241–51.

Ross, Lawrence J. "Symbol and Structure in the *Secunda pastorum.*" *Medieval English Drama.* Edited by Jerome Taylor and Alan Nelson. Chicago: University of Chicago Press, 1972.

Rossiter, A. P. *English Drama from Early Times to the Elizabethans.* London: Hutchinson's University Library, 1950.

Salter, F. M. *Mediaeval Drama in Chester.* Toronto: University of Toronto Press, 1955.

Sanders, Barry, "Who's Afraid of Jesus Christ? Games in the *Coliphizacio.*" *Comparative Drama* 2 (1968):94–99.

Singleton, Charles. "Dante's Allegory." *Speculum* 25 (1950):76–86.

Southern, Richard. *The Medieval Theatre in the Round.* London: Faber & Faber, 1957.

Speirs, John. "The Towneley Shepherds' Plays." In *A Guide to English Literature,* vol. 1, edited by Boris Ford. London: Penguin, 1954.

Stevens, Martin. "Illusion and Reality in the Medieval Drama." *College English* 32 (1971):448–64.

———. "The Manuscript of the Towneley Plays: Its History and Editions." *Papers of the Bibliographical Society of America* 67 (1973):231–44.

———. "The Theatre of the World: A Study in Medieval Dramatic Form." *Chaucer Review* 7 (1972):234–49.

Thompson, Francis. "Unity in *The Second Shepherds' Tale.*" *MLN* 64 (1949):302–6.

Thompson, Stith. *Motif Index of Folk-literature.* Vol 4. Bloomington: Indiana University Press, 1955.

Utley, Francis Lee. *The Crooked Rib*. Columbus: Ohio State University Press, 1944.

Vignaux, Paul. *Philosophy in the Middle Ages*. New York: Meridien, 1959.

Watt, Homer. "The Dramatic Unity of the *Secunda pastorum*." In *Essays and Studies in Honor of Carleton Brown*. New York: New York University Press, 1940.

Weimann, Robert. "Realismus und Simultankonvention im Misteriendrama: Mimesis, Parodie und Utopie in den Towneley-Hirtenszene." *Shakespeare Jahrbuch* 103 (1967): 108–35.

Whitesell, J. E. "Chaucer's Lisping Friar." *MLN* 71 (1956):160–61.

Wickham, Glynne. *Early English Stages*. 2 vols. London: Routledge & Kegan Paul, 1951.

Williams, Arnold. *The Drama of Medieval England*. East Lansing, Mich.: Michigan State University Press, 1968.

————. "Typology and the Cycle Plays: Some Criteria." *Speculum* 43 (1968):677–84.

Woolf, Rosemary. *The English Mystery Plays*. Berkeley: University of California Press, 1972.

Young, Karl. *Drama of the Medieval Church*. 2 vols. Oxford: Clarendon Press, 1933.

Zumwalt, Eugene. "Irony of the Towneley Shepherds' Plays." *Research Studies of the State College of Washington* 26 (1968):37–53.

Index